The Ultimate HEALTHY HOMEMADE SLOW COOKER DOG FOOD Cookbook

Parker Tanner

© Copyright 2024 - All rights reserved.

The content contained within this book may not be reproduced, duplicated or transmitted without direct written permission from the author or the publisher.

Under no circumstances will any blame or legal responsibility be held against the publisher, or author, for any damages, reparation, or monetary loss due to the information contained within this book, either directly or indirectly.

Legal Notice:

This book is copyright protected. It is only for personal use. You cannot amend, distribute, sell, use, quote or paraphrase any part of the content within this book without the consent of the author or publisher.

Disclaimer Notice:

Please note the information contained within this document is for educational and entertainment purposes only. All effort has been executed to present accurate, up to date, reliable, complete information. No warranties of any kind are declared or implied. Readers acknowledge that the author is not engaged in the rendering of legal, financial, medical or professional advice. The content within this book has been derived from various sources. Please consult a licensed professional before attempting any techniques outlined in this book.

By reading this document, the reader agrees that under no circumstances is the author responsible for any losses, direct or indirect, that are incurred as a result of the use of the information contained within this document, including, but not limited to, errors, omissions, or inaccuracies.

PARKER TANNER

Contents

CONTENTS	3
INTRODUCTION	6
UNDERSTANDING YOUR DOG'S DIETARY NEEDS	9
THE ART OF SLOW COOKING	15
BUILDING A BALANCED MEAL	18
BUDGET-FRIENDLY COOKING	22
ADDRESSING DIETARY CHALLENGES	26
TROUBLESHOOTING AND TIPS	30
ENSURING NUTRITIONAL BALANCE	33
SIMPLE AND NUTRITIOUS EVERYDAY MEALS	37
TAIL-WAGGING TURKEY & SWEET POTATO STEW	38
BARKING BEEF & BARLEY DELIGHT	39
PUPPY LOVE CHICKEN & RICE MEDLEY	40
FURRY FRIEND FISH & POTATO FEAST	41
CANINE COMFORT LAMB & LENTIL STEW	42
WAG-WORTHY CHICKEN & PUMPKIN DELIGHT	43
BEEFY CARROT & SPINACH SUPER STEW	44
PUPPY PLEASER APPLE & PORK MEDLEY	45
HAPPY HOUND BEEF & GREEN BEAN CASSEROLE	46
BOW-WOW BEEF & BLUEBERRY BOOST	47
SWEET POTATO & CHICKEN COMFORT BOWL	48
BALANCED BEEF & BARLEY BLEND	49
DOGGY DREAM BEEF & BROCCOLI DINNER	50
CHICKEN & VEGGIE SUPREME	51
SALMON & SPINACH OMEGA BOOST	52
ALL-DOG BEEF & PUMPKIN MASH	53
BEEF & APPLE AUTUMN HARVEST	54
PORK & PEAR HARVEST MIX	55
SALMON & SWEET POTATO DELIGHT	56
PUMPKIN & CHICKEN DIGESTIVE DELIGHT	57
QUICK-PREP OPTIONS FOR BUSY DAYS	58
PAWS-ITIVELY PERFECT CHICKEN & BROWN RICE BOWL	59
TAIL-WAGGING TURKEY & VEGGIE MEDLEY	60
WOOF-WORTHY BEEF & BARLEY BLISS	61
SPEEDY SALMON & POTATO POWER-UP	62
FAST & FLUFFY TURKEY & PUMPKIN CHOW	63
QUICK BEEF & SWEET PEA MASH	64
CHICKEN & SPINACH EXPRESS DELIGHT	65
SPEEDY PORK & APPLE MASH-UP	66
SALMON & BLUEBERRY BOOSTER BOWL	67
TURBO TURKEY & BUTTERNUT SQUASH CHOW	68
PORK & PUMPKIN PERFECT STEW	69
EXPRESS BEEF & SPINACH STEW	70
QUICK COD & PUMPKIN STEW	71
FAST LAMB & GREEN BEAN CASSEROLE	72
SALMON & SWEET POTATO DELIGHT	73
RAPID CHICKEN & KALE DINNER	74
UNIVERSAL TURKEY & BROWN RICE DELIGHT	75
TAIL-WAG TURKEY & BLUEBERRY TREAT	76
WOOF-WORTHY BEEF & BARLEY BLISS	77
SPEEDY PORK & PEAR MASH-UP	78
VERSATILE RECIPES FOR ALL DOGS	79

All-Pup Lamb & Sweet Potato Stew	80
Universal Beef & Barley Chow	81
Mighty Meat & Veggie Mix	82
Happy Paws Chicken & Oat Stew	83
Pooch Perfect Turkey & Spinach Stew	84
Salmon & Sweet Pea Power Bowl	85
Balanced Beef & Apple Supreme	86
Ultimate Chicken & Green Bean Chowder	87
Mighty Meal Lamb & Lentil Mix	88
Pumpkin & Chicken Digestive Delight	89
All-In-One Beef & Veggie Feast	90
Rapid Lamb & Barley Mix	91
Salmon & Veggie Omega Bowl	92
Turkey & Sweet Potato Sensation	93
Pork & Pear Hearty Harvest	94
Bark & Bite Beefy Lentil Stew	95
Turkey & Spinach Super Mix	96
Salmon & Kale Omega Boost	97
Chicken & Sweet Pea Supreme	98
Lamb & Lentil Power Bowl	99

GRAIN-FREE & GLUTEN-FREE OPTIONS 100

Grain-Free Gobbler's Delight	101
Sweet Potato Salmon Sensation	102
Pumpkin & Turkey Primal Feast	103
Pawsome Paleo Pork & Apple Stew	104
Coconut Chicken Grain-Free Comfort	105
Veggie-Loaded Beef Paleo Stew	106
Quinoa-Free Kale & Cod Casserole	107
Gluten-Free Turkey & Blueberry Boost	108
Cranberry Chicken Caveman Chow	109
Pea & Lamb Protein-Packed Bowl	110
No-Grain Beef & Spinach Supreme	111
Wild Salmon & Butternut Squash Bake	112
Carrot-Coconut Paleo Power Stew	113
Hunter's Hearty Grain-Free Mix	114
Sweet Pea & Turkey Caveman Casserole	115
Apple & Pork Paleo Comfort Meal	116
Wild-Caught Cod & Cauliflower Chowder	117
Beef & Kale Primal Feast	118
Bone Broth & Pumpkin Paleo Potluck	119
Herb-Infused Grain-Free Chicken Dinner	120

LOW-FAT & LOW-CALORIE MEALS 121

Slim & Trim Turkey & Carrot Medley	122
Light & Lean Chicken Veggie Bowl	123
Calorie-Conscious Beef & Broccoli Blend	124
Skinny Salmon & Spinach Delight	125
Lightened-Up Lamb & Lentil Stew	126
Guilt-Free Sweet Potato & Apple Treat	127
Skinny Chicken & Zucchini Hash	128
Lean Green Bean & Turkey Supreme	129
Low-Calorie Cod & Kale Mash-Up	130
Svelte Sweet Potato & Pork Mash	131
Lite Bite Beef & Pumpkin Platter	132
Skinny Veggie & Turkey Fit Feast	133
Calorie Cutter Chicken & Apple Mix	134
Low-Fat Lamb & Carrot Surprise	135
Wholesome Waistline Chicken Chowder	136
Lean Green Turkey & Pea Stew	137
Trimmed-Down Beef & Spinach Bowl	138
Slim Salmon & Blueberry Mix	139
Low-Cal Lamb & Lentil Love	140
Lite Liver & Veggie Dinner	141

SPECIAL HEALTH NEEDS 142

Sensitive Stomach Sweet Potato & Cod Stew	143
Joint Support Chicken & Pumpkin Blend	144
Heart-Healthy Turkey & Beet Bowl	145
Anti-Inflammatory Beef & Turmeric Mash	146
Skin & Coat Salmon & Flaxseed Feast	147

Digestive Boost Pumpkin & Pork Stew	148
Kidney-Friendly Lamb & Quinoa Mix	149
Low-Allergen Turkey & Green Bean Bowl	150
Immune Support Chicken & Kale Blend	151
Diabetic-Friendly Beef & Lentil Medley	152
Liver Care Lamb & Sweet Potato Stew	153
Omega-Boost Salmon & Chia Supper	154
High-Fiber Chicken & Carrot Digestive Delight	155
Senior Dog Beef & Pumpkin Comfort Mix	156
Urinary Support Turkey & Cranberry Stew	157
Allergy Relief Duck-Free Delight	158
Weight Management Pork & Spinach Blend	159
Bone Health Turkey & Sardine Casserole	160
Low-Sodium Chicken & Rice Recovery Meal	161
Inflammation Fighter Beef & Blueberry Bowl	162

HOMEMADE BISCUITS AND CHEWS — 163

Crunchy Carrot & Apple Biscuits	164
Peanut Butter Banana Bites	165
Sweet Potato Chewies	166
Cheesy Chicken Bites	167
Pumpkin & Parsley Breath Fresheners	168
Apple Cinnamon Crunchies	169
Blueberry Bliss Bites	170
Sweet Potato & Salmon Chews	171
Cheddar & Parsley Breath Biscuits	172
Pumpkin & Oat Crunchies	173

SPECIAL OCCASION TREATS — 174

Birthday Pupcake Delight	175
Peanut Butter & Pumpkin Party Balls	176
Apple & Bacon Celebration Bites	177
Carob & Banana Party Cookies	178
Festive Cranberry & Turkey Treats	179
Honey & Oat Celebration Bars	180
Savory Cheese & Bacon Bites	181
Sweet Potato & Coconut Festive Chews	182
Banana & Yogurt Party Drops	183
Cranberry & Chicken Celebration Bites	184
Birthday Pupcake Delight	185
Peanut Butter & Pumpkin Party Balls	186
Apple & Bacon Celebration Bites	187
Carob & Banana Party Cookies	188
Festive Cranberry & Turkey Treats	189
Honey & Oat Celebration Bars	190
Savory Cheese & Bacon Bites	191
Sweet Potato & Coconut Festive Chews	192
Banana & Yogurt Party Drops	193
Cranberry & Chicken Celebration Bites	194

TRAINING REWARDS & SNACKS — 195

Chicken & Cheese Training Tidbits	196
Peanut Butter & Carrot Nibbles	197
Turkey & Blueberry Mini Bites	198
Salmon & Sweet Potato Training Treats	199
Apple & Pumpkin Training Nuggets	200
Coconut & Banana Training Bites	201
Beef & Carrot Mini Morsels	202
Sweet Potato & Peanut Butter Training Tots	203
Turkey & Cranberry Nibbles	204
Pumpkin & Apple Training Bites	205

GLOSSARY — 206

REFERENCES — 207

Introduction

Do you feel guilty when you dig into a flavorful, nutritious meal at the end of a long day while your dog must make do with a bowl of kibble made from dubious ingredients? Gone are the days when we naively believed chicken-flavored dog food was made from real chicken and designed with your puppy's health in mind. Companies cut corners and use low-quality, ultra-process ingredients to chase profits, and your dog's health and longevity may suffer as a result. If you want to change your dog's begging puppy eyes into a look of health, happiness, and satisfaction, this book will help you achieve your goal.

Welcome to the world of homemade dog food! You'll discover everything you need to provide your dog with nutritionally balanced, safe, and tasty meals free of industrial toxins and tailored to your dog's specific dietary needs. All the meals and treats in this book aim to enhance your dog's quality of life without being a burden on your time or wallet. You'll find specific instructions, nutritional analyses, and details about portion sizes to take the guesswork out of feeding time. Explore the benefits of home cooking for your dog, why slow cooking is the best option for preserving nutrients, and how you can strengthen your special bond with your fur baby through shared meals.

We kick off **Chapter 1** with a detailed look at your dog's dietary needs. You'll find helpful dog-specific information on proteins, fats, fiber, and carbohydrates, followed by a section about essential vitamins and minerals for canines and an examination of hydration and its importance. The chapter also discusses how to tailor diets to individual dogs. We'll look at age-specific nutritional needs, how to adjust diet for activity levels, and special considerations for various dog breeds.

The art of slow cooking is our focus for **Chapter 2**. We explore why slow cooking works best for dog food with sections explaining how slow cooking retains flavors and nutrients, why it is convenient and makes preparation a breeze, and the advantages of slow cooking for batch cooking. Then, we learn how to master slow cooking techniques. Become a slow cooking guru by reading the sections about laying ingredients, tips on timing and temperature, and troubleshooting common issues.

Chapter 3 is all about building a balanced meal. Craft and create complete and nutritious recipes by balancing proteins, carbohydrates, and fats, incorporating the right veggies and grains, and using supplements wisely. When you know what makes a meal balanced, you can personalize meals for your dog. Discover how to modify meals according to allergies and sensitivities, enhance the flavor with dog-safe ingredients, and create variety by including seasonal produce.

Quality dog food doesn't have to break the bank. In **Chapter 4**, we put budget-friendly cooking under the microscope. We start by examining cost-effective ingredient choices. Get helpful tips on how to find affordable protein sources, how to utilize bulk grains and vegetables, and how to shop smartly at local markets. Put this knowledge to use with a section about maximizing efficiency in meal prep, where we discuss batch cooking and freezing techniques, how to streamline grocery shopping, and how to utilize leftovers creatively.

Address dietary challenges in **Chapter 5**, where we discover how to enhance meal appeal. Make your dog drool by boosting flavors naturally, adding textures dogs love, and rotating recipes to keep your dog interested. We also discuss the challenges of allergies and sensitivities. You'll find information about identifying common allergens, safe ingredient substitutions, and monitoring your dog's reactions.

Ensure your homemade dog meals go smoothly with **Chapter 6's** troubleshooting and tips. We solve common cooking problems by fixing consistency issues, adjusting flavors, and salvaging overcooked or undercooked meals. Stay informed and inspired and become part of the home cooking movement by keeping up with nutrition trends, engaging with dog nutrition communities, and continuing education for optimal pet health.

In **Chapter 7**, we look at nutritional compliance to help your home-cooked food meet the highest standards. We start with the AAFCO guidelines and explore the key nutrient profiles for dogs, how to meet AAFCO standards in homemade meals, and the importance of complete and balanced diets. Then, we discuss WSAVA Global Nutrition Committee insights regarding core nutritional recommendations, tailoring diets to meet global standards, and consulting with veterinary nutritionists. The chapter finishes with a section on balancing homemade meals, where we explore the use of supplements to fill nutritional gaps, regular assessment of your dog's health, and how to adjust recipes for nutritional compliance.

The recipe section of this book starts in **Chapter 8**, where you'll find basic recipes for simple and nutritious everyday meals, quick-prep options for busy days, and versatile recipes suitable for all dogs.

Chapter 9 contains special diet recipes, including grain-free and gluten-free meals, low-fat and low-calorie options for dogs who need to watch their waistlines, and recipes for dogs with specific health needs.

Bring wags to your dog's tail with the treat's recipes in **Chapter 10**. There are recipes for homemade biscuits and chews, special occasion treats, and training rewards and snacks.

The book ends with bonus material that includes a 30-day meal plan with balanced and varied foods, as well as helpful charts. You'll find charts to help you determine portion sizes, various toppers you can add to meals, treats that pair well with meals, and a measuring chart to ensure accuracy for meal consistency.

Let's jump in and start our journey with an exploration of your dog's dietary needs.

1

Understanding Your Dog's Dietary Needs

Food is more than a tasty morsel to please our tastebuds and prevent hunger pangs. Living beings depend on food to provide and maintain energy, fuel bodily processes, and ensure health. However, not all foods are equal across species. What is good for the goose may be good for the gander but not for humans, and what is needed on the human plate isn't necessarily healthy in the dog's bowl. In this chapter, we'll explore the key nutrients needed to keep your dog in top condition and how to tailor diets to the needs of individual dogs.

Key Nutrients for Canine Health

Before we can put together a meal for our dogs, we need to understand what nutrients should be in their food. We'll discuss the correct ratios and amounts of nutrients later in this chapter.

Proteins, Fats, Fiber, and Carbohydrates

The exact proportions of the nutrients in the title and all their benefits for dogs are still somewhat under dispute by experts. Although dog nutrition sources differ in the details, some facts are universally accepted, and these are the ones we'll discuss.

The types of protein differ according to the variation of amino acids from which they are made. There are 22 amino acids used by dogs, and since they can't manufacture many of them, their bodies must source the amino acids from their food. Amino acids build proteins that become hormones, secretions, tendons, ligaments, muscles, and enzymes. A good protein source for your dog must contain amino acids your dog requires and must be easily digestible. Some proteins often found in commercial dog food, such as gelatin, byproducts, cereal waste, poor quality meat, and collagen, can't supply all the amino acids a dog needs to fully thrive. The best protein sources for canines are dairy, eggs, and lean meats. Dogs can also benefit from plant-based protein from grains and legumes.

Dogs need two types of fats to thrive: fatty acids and triglycerides. Triglycerides give your dog energy, cushion internal organs, maintain body heat, provide structure to cells, and help in the movement of molecules in the body. Fatty acids are responsible for your dog's lustrous coat, healthy skin, proper brain and eye development, and the lowering of inflammation. The fatty acids that your dog's body can't produce and must be sourced from food are called essential fatty acids, such as Omega-6 and Omega-3. Healthy sources of fat for your canine companion include flaxseed oil, fish oil, and the fat of beef and chicken.

Fiber is often overlooked, which can result in digestive issues. Dog food should include soluble fiber (it can dissolve in water), which is beneficial for intestinal bacteria, as well as insoluble fiber. Insoluble fiber helps keep your dog feeling full for longer, aids in the formation of feces, and prevents constipation. A healthy digestive system helps prevent the development of anal gland inflammation.

Because domestic dogs are related to wolves, and wolves can't digest and process carbohydrates very well, some people believe that dogs don't benefit from carbohydrates. However, our family dogs have more genes for an enzyme that enables them to digest carbohydrates. Dogs that can't tolerate a high-protein diet or are pregnant or lactating thrive when well-prepared carbohydrates are added to their diets.

Essential Vitamins and Minerals

Without the right vitamins, your dog loses out on optimal bone and hormonal health, proper wound healing, strong bones, and healthy joints and gums. Here are the vitamins your dog's diet should include:

- vitamin B, including vitamin B1 (thiamine), vitamin B2 (riboflavin), vitamin B3 (nicotinic acid or niacin), vitamin B5 (pantothenic acid), vitamin B6 (pyridoxine), vitamin B9 (folic acid), and vitamin B12 (cobalamin)
- choline is a substance that isn't technically a vitamin or mineral but functions similarly in the body to vitamin B
- vitamin A (retinol)
- vitamin D (cholecalciferol)
- vitamin E (tocopherol)
- vitamin K (phylloquinone)

Minerals are vital in bone and teeth health, regulating body fluids, and processing food into energy. Your dog only needs small amounts of the following trace minerals:

- zinc
- Iodine
- fluorine
- chromium
- selenium
- iron
- copper
- manganese

Make sure your dog's diet contains plenty of these macrominerals:

- magnesium
- potassium
- calcium
- sodium
- sulfur
- chloride

Hydration and Its Importance

- Having plenty of fresh water always available is essential for these biological processes in your dog:
- Keeping up energy levels. One of the first signs of dehydration is a lethargic god with little stamina.
- Preventing heatstroke. Heatstroke can be deadly to your dog. Proper hydration is needed for your dog to cool down through panting and paw-pad sweating.
- Maintaining urinary health. Adequate water intake lowers the risk of bladder stones, urinary crystals, and urinary tract infections.
- Smooth joint function. Without proper hydration, joints can't have adequate lubrication.
- Optimal muscle function. When a dog's hydration drops too low, muscles tend to cramp and ache.
- Efficient digestion. Water is crucial for digestion and the uptake of nutrients. Low hydration can lead to constipation and indigestion.
- Cognitive function. Your dog's brain needs adequate hydration to perform at its best. If hydration levels are too low, the dog can become disoriented and confused.
- Maintaining healthy skin and coat. Dogs without proper hydration levels don't have shiny coats, and their skin may be flaky and dry.

- Getting rid of toxins. Dogs excrete toxins via the urine. Keep your dog detoxed with good hydration to support the kidneys.

Tailoring Diets to Individual Dogs

Age-Specific Nutritional Needs

Senior dogs will need these adjustments to their diets:

- More dietary fiber to prevent constipation.
- Less fiber if the dog has a condition that affects the absorption of nutrients.
- Increased beta-carotene and vitamins E and C to combat age-related oxidative stress and improve immunity.
- Improved protein quality since they can't process as effectively as younger dogs.
- More polyunsaturated fatty acids since the body's natural production of these substances decrease with age.
- More organic salts containing manganese, iron, zinc, and copper for coat and skin health.
- Older dogs are prone to dental issues. Their food should be soft and easier to chew.
- Puppies need three times as much calcium and four times more protein than a fully grown dog.

Adjusting for Activity Levels

Working, young, or very active dogs need more energy-rich diets with plenty of carbohydrates and muscle-repairing protein.

Dogs who are inactive due to arthritis can benefit from added glucosamine, hydrolyzed collagen, chondroitin sulfate, and polyphenols.

Dogs who are inactive due to illness or arthritis need lower-energy diets to avoid becoming overweight.

Special Considerations for Dog Breeds

Although it isn't necessary to have a breed-specific diet if your dog gets high-quality, balanced food, some considerations can be important:

- German shepherds tend to have digestive issues, which can be kept in check with low-fat meats and high-fiber foods such as fresh vegetables and seeds.
- Rottweilers, pit bulls, and dobermans can benefit from pre-biotic and probiotic supplements and high-protein diets.
- Short hair breeds often need extra copper and zinc.
- Long-hair breeds can be at risk of overheating, and thus, hydration and electrolytes should be monitored.
- Labrador retrievers require a diet with 30% protein, with the rest made up of fiber, carbohydrates, and fats.
- Golden retrievers require a 25% protein diet with moderate carbohydrates as well as foods high in omega-3 fatty acids.
- Poodles do best on a diet with plenty of low-fat meat, fish, and fresh veggies.
- Ibizan hounds may develop neurological issues without a diet high in nickel.
- Schnauzers and dalmatians thrive on diets that include some good-quality oats, wheat, barley, or other grains.
- Maltese diets should contain a minimum of 25% fiber from good-quality legumes, whole grains, veggies, and fruits.
- Akitas requires high-fat diets.
- Jack Russel terriers need vitamin A for healthy bones and skin but in lower amounts than other breeds.
- Bulldogs need fiber-rich diets to help prevent diabetes.
- Border collies need low-sodium diets for proper water balance.
- Beagles tend to develop kidney issues on high-protein diets.

In the next chapter, we'll discover the art of slow cooking for preparing your own dog food.

2

The Art of Slow Cooking

Slow cooking is an easy and convenient way to prepare flavorful, nutritious meals for your furry friend. In this chapter, you'll find all the information you need to become a dog food master chef.

Why Slow Cooking Works for Dog Food

Not only is slow cooking incredibly easy and it results in foods guaranteed to make your dog drool and stay healthy, but this method also produces foods that can be safely refrigerated.

Retaining Flavors and Nutrients

Because slow cooking has ingredients simmering for long periods, the food has time to properly soak up flavors. Meat becomes more tender, which is ideal for older dogs or young dogs with dental problems. Because nutrients aren't damaged by high heat, food retains its nutritious value.

Convenience and Ease of Preparation

Slow cooking offers you the freedom of not having to stand watch over pots. Despite the cooker working for hours, it still uses less electricity than stove-top cooking. The chance of burning food in a slow cooker's lower temperatures is greatly reduced. As a bonus, a slow cooker cuts down on dishes and is very easy to clean.

Perfect for Batch Cooking

Due to the ease of slow cooking and retention of nutrients, you can prepare meals in advance. Batch cooking means you don't have to cook every day and always have a meal ready to defrost, which gives you more free time.

Mastering Slow Cooker Techniques

Liquid remains in the cooker, so you don't have to add extra liquid throughout the cooking process. In this section, you'll find more helpful tips on mastering slow cooking.

Layering Ingredients for Best Results

The slow cooker heats from the bottom, so you get the most even cooking when you put the ingredients that take the longest to cook, such as carrots and potatoes, at the bottom. The next layer is meat, topped with vegetables that cook fairly quickly, such as onions.

If you add cheese or other dairy products, do so as the top layer close to the end of cooking time.

Timing and Temperature Tips

Use the low-temperature setting for general cooking and the high-temperature only when the recipe demands.

Don't leave food in a switched-off slow cooker for long periods to avoid the temperature range optimal for harmful bacteria (39–140 °F or 4–60 °C).

Troubleshooting Common Issues

Add your pasta or rice near the end of cooking otherwise they can develop an unappetizing texture.

Every time you lift the slow cooker's lid, heat escapes. Compensate by cooking an extra 15 minutes for every lift.

If your food comes out too thin, thicken it with a paste made with two tablespoons of cornstarch and water.

The next chapter will help you build a balanced meal for your fur family.

3

Building a Balanced Meal

In this chapter, you'll find information to help you craft a meal with all the nutrients and tastiness your dog needs, as well as how to cope with food allergies, make meals tastier, and add variety.

Crafting Complete and Nutritious Recipes

To plan a recipe that will satisfy all the dietary requirements your dog needs for optimal health, you must consider the balance between nutrients, the role of carbohydrates, and the addition of supplements.

Balancing Proteins, Carbohydrates, and Fat

Active dogs and puppies need more protein than older or less active dogs. Good sources of protein for a doggy diet include fish, eggs, and meat.

Carbohydrates in the form of veggies and grains should be given only in moderate portions. Pregnant and lactating dogs do best with a little extra carbohydrate.

Adding fish oil, chicken fat, and flaxseed oil to your dog food provides omega-3 and omega-6 fatty acids. All fats are energy-dense, so adjust according to your dog's activity level. The more active they are, the more fat your dog can eat without becoming overweight.

The National Research Council suggests the following guidelines per 1000 calories for dogs 12 months and older (NRC Nutritional Requirements for Dogs, Dog Nutrition, Raw Feeding, n.d.)

Nutrient	Recommended Allowance	Portion
Protein	25 g	20 g minimum
Fat	14 g	82 g minimum

There aren't current carbohydrate recommendations since adult dogs can get their glucose from fats and certain amino acids through a process called gluconeogenesis. However, adding carbohydrates adds valuable fiber to a dog's diet.

Incorporating Vegetables and Grains

Ensure your dog's energy and fiber needs are provided for by incorporating vegetables such as peas, carrots, and sweet potatoes and dog-friendly whole grains such as barley, oats, and brown rice.

Be aware that some dogs might have food sensitivity to some veggies or grains. If you notice any constipation, bloating, vomiting, or loose stool, change the ingredients.

Using Supplements Wisely

Too many supplements can be harmful to your dog. If you are using more than a general conditioning tablet, or if your dog has a health condition or is pregnant or lactating, please consult your vet about which supplements would be beneficial.

Personalizing Your Dog's Diet

Modifying for Allergies and Sensitivities

Allergies and sensitivities result from triggers to your dog's immune system. Keep in mind that allergies can take months or years to develop, so it is very possible that your dog may develop an allergy to a food that has been part of their diet for a long time. Food intolerances may develop very quickly, and reactions to abnormal or spoiled food may happen almost immediately after eating (such as vomiting after feasting on the contents of a trash can).

Your vet can help you draw up an elimination diet or test for allergens to find exactly what foods your dog is sensitive or allergic to. Symptoms that a particular type of food doesn't agree with your dog's immune system include a dull coat, flaky, itchy, or dry skin, an upset stomach, or chronic infections.

Enhancing Flavors with Dog-Safe Ingredients

Add the following dog-safe ingredients to make your dog's meals tastier:

- Pureed pumpkin is a natural sweetener that most dogs love, and it provides extra fiber.
- Artificial meat flavoring from a source that honors the FDA regulations.
- Nutritious and tasty bone broth, especially unsalted chicken broth, can make Dog food more appealing.
- Many dogs find cheese irresistible.
- Most picky eaters will wag their tails for some unsweetened, unsalted peanut butter. Be warned that the artificial sweetener xylitol, which is found in many peanut butter brands, is harmful to dogs.

Creating Variety with Seasonal Produce

Keep your dog's food from becoming boring by adding seasonal fruits, berries, and vegetables that are healthy for your dog:

In **summer**, add cantaloupe or seedless watermelon, zucchini, green beans, or small portions of lightly cooked bell peppers.

Fall is for sweet potatoes, seedless apples, brussels sprouts, and pumpkins.

Enhance **winter** recipes with added kale, spinach, parsnip, beet, and carrots. Cranberries are sweet treats full of antioxidants but high in sugar, so give only small amounts to your dog.

Spring produce includes peas, blueberries, and asparagus.

Remember to include new produce gradually in the meals to avoid upset tummies.

Join me in the next chapter for tips on how to create budget-friendly meals for your wet-nosed companion.

4

Budget-Friendly Cooking

Home cooking your dog's meals ensures a diet packed with the right nutrients. As an added bonus to preparing the meals yourself, you'll save money! In this chapter, we'll explore how home cooking your own dog food affects your wallet.

Cost-Effective Ingredient Choices

Although your dog might appreciate an occasional share of your steak, you can meet their dietary needs with less expensive options. In this section, we'll explore some ways in which you can keep costs down.

Affordable Protein Sources

Poor quality protein may not supply all the amino acids your dog needs, so aim for the best quality you can comfortably afford with these tips:

- Good-quality meat may be expensive, so save money by buying in bulk and keeping an eye out for sales.
- Bone broth can be made with skin, bones, and connective tissue. Look for off-cuts at your local butchery.
- Chicken and turkey are excellent sources of protein that won't break the bank.

Utilizing Bulk Grains and Vegetables

Buy vegetables in bulk and divide them into smaller packets that can be frozen and taken out as needed. Remember to freeze in airtight containers, and if any mold grows on your veggies or grains, toss them into the trash. Moldy or spoiled food isn't suitable for dogs.

Shopping Smart at Local Markets

The best and most affordable ingredients may be only a block or two away. Keep these hints in mind when you go shopping:

- Some stores offer DIY dog food kits with recipes and pre-measured ingredients. These kits may work out to be less expensive than buying the ingredients separately.
- You might find bargains on ingredients at your local farmer's market.
- Locally sourced ingredients are often less expensive than those that are shipped or trucked.

Maximizing Efficiency in Meal Prep

Shopping, cooking, freezing, and dealing with leftovers can be overwhelming. In this section, we explore ways of making these tasks easy and efficient.

Batch Cooking and Freezing Techniques

Here are some helpful tips for mastering batch cooking and freezing your dog food:

- Make technology work for you and use a food processor instead of chopping up bundles of green beans or heaps of pumpkin.
- After cooking, let the dog food cool down first before going into the freezer.

- Put a layer of baking paper on top of the food in an airtight container to prevent the ice crystals, known as freezer, burn.
- Leave some space in your freezer for air to circulate. This makes your freezer more effective.
- Use labels to show when you made the food so that you use the older foods first.
- When defrosting, leave the container in the fridge overnight instead of leaving it out, which may be an invitation to harmful bacteria.

Streamlining Grocery Shopping

Save time and money when you go shopping with these helpful hints:

- Decide which recipes you want to use and make a list of the ingredients. If you try to remember instead of writing it down, you might forget items or buy unneeded ingredients.
- Organize your shopping list by aisle to save time by reducing backtracking.
- Look at store ads to hunt for specials and discounts and use coupons.
- When buying vegetables, compare the fresh ones with pre-cut, packed items. The fresh, unpacked ones are usually less expensive.

Utilizing Leftovers Creatively

Throwing leftovers in the trash is wasting an opportunity to be creative. Let's look at some creative ideas for leftovers:

- Turn dog food leftovers into treats by adding mashed banana and peanut butter, dividing and shaping the mixture into small balls, and baking for 10 minutes at 350 °F (180 °C). Give the cooled-down treats as a healthy snack.
- Contact your local animal shelter or rescue to donate the leftovers. Many shelters and rescuers will pick donations up at your residence.
- Become an animal hero by leaving leftovers for strays.
- Mix leftovers into your compost pile to add nutrients that your garden will love. In the next chapter, we'll find solutions to common dietary challenges.

5

Addressing Dietary Challenges

In this chapter, we'll place dietary challenges under the microscope to ensure your meals are appealing and safe.

Enhancing Meal Appeal

Dogs can be picky eaters. Like humans, they have their particular likes and dislikes. This section will help you cater to your dog's preferences to have them salivating in anticipation at every meal.

Boosting Flavors Naturally

We've seen in a previous chapter that you can add cheese, bone broth, pumpkin, and meat flavoring to make meals more enticing. Here are more tips on how to make dog food more tempting:

- Mix in a little warm water to enhance the aroma and taste.
- A little plain yogurt added to the bowl can tempt most dogs.
- Add your cooked meat leftovers or unwanted parts, such as the skin and organs, to the dog food.

- Wet your dog's appetite with the addition of an unsalted scrambled or boiled egg.

Adding Textures Dogs Love

Kibble and bones help keep dogs' teeth clean, which is why dogs naturally enjoy a little extra texture now and then. Here are some ways you can use dog-healthy food to add texture to meals:

- Add a little grated raw carrot for crunch.
- Thinly sliced celery supplies fiber and crunch.
- Many dogs enjoy the texture of cooked oatmeal mixed into their food.
- A spoonful of flax seeds adds texture and healthy omega-3 fatty acids.
- Cooked liver is a nutritious, chewy addition.

Rotating Recipes to Maintain Interest

Would you enjoy eating the same food every day? Just like you, your dog appreciates variation to keep meals from being boring. Prepare a couple of different meals and label them before freezing. This way, it is easy and convenient to defrost and serve up the variation that your dog will love.

Managing Allergies and Sensitivities

This section will help you spot the symptoms of allergies and how you can adjust your dog's diet to make it safe.

Identifying Common Allergens

The foods most likely to cause allergies in dogs are soy, egg yolk, wheat, beef, chicken, dairy, lamb, and chicken.

Keep an eye on your dog's health and behavior. If your dog keeps scratching, licking a paw or has any other symptom listed at the end of this section, you can start an elimination diet to find out if a specific food is a cause. Simply eliminate a certain ingredient from your dog's diet for a couple of days and see if the symptoms go away.

Safe Ingredient Substitutions

Eliminating ingredients or having the vet run an allergy test are the easiest ways to detect the cause of an allergy. Once you have identified the food allergen, you can substitute the following ingredients:

- Consider alternative good-quality protein sources such as fish, venison, duck, or turkey.
- Instead of grains, use lentils, peas, pumpkin, or sweet potatoes as fiber sources.
- Tofu and quinoa are non-allergenic, easily digestible, and add protein to meals.

- If your dog has an egg allergy, replace eggs in the recipes with yogurt or mashed banana. These ingredients have the same binding qualities as eggs.
- You can also substitute dairy with coconut milk and wheat with brown rice.
- Sometimes, the cooking method can contribute to allergies. If you are frying the food, try steaming or baking it instead.

Monitoring Your Dog's Reactions

If your dog has any of the following symptoms, a food allergy may be the culprit: itchiness, especially on paws

- vomiting
- skin rash
- ear infection
- scaly, leathery, or oily skin
- sneezing
- red eyes
- hair that falls out
- eye discharge

Some symptoms may indicate more serious issues, and you should contact your vet if your dog has severe diarrhea, vomiting, infection, or lethargy. Let's head over to the next chapter for troubleshooting and tips.

6

Troubleshooting and Tips

When you have trouble with your dog food consistency and flavor, or if your food ends up raw or overdone, all isn't lost! This chapter will help fix common cooking problems, as well as give ideas on how to stay up to date with new developments in the world of dog food home cooking.

Solving Common Cooking Problems

Even an experienced chef may need to troubleshoot on occasion. In this section, we'll look at some of the most common issues that may pop up in your kitchen.

Fixing Consistency Issues

A slow cooker, with the lid on, creates a closed system where juices and steam accumulate and do not evaporate. As a result, the liquid doesn't reduce and will stay watery. Thicken your dish with a mixture of one part tapioca starch or cornstarch to two parts cold water and turn the heat up for about 15 minutes. When you use a slow cooker, you only need to add about a cup of water and not keep topping up the water level.

Adjust Flavors Appropriately

Sear your meat in a pan before putting it in your slow cooker. This will help preserve texture and flavor. Also, vegetables that cook too long can become soggy and tasteless. If you plan to leave your slow cooker on all day, it may be wise to wait a few hours before adding the veggies. Vegetables high in fiber, such as carrots, can be added at the start of cooking, but delicate veggies, such as peas, should be held back until later.

Salvaging Undercooked or Overcooked Meals

If you pack your slow cooker too full, some ingredients may end up overcooked and others undercooked. Avoid this by only filling your slow cooker three-quarters full.

Staying Informed and Inspired

Society makes progress every day, not only with technology and industry but also with nutrition. The more scientists discover about dogs, the better we can care for and feed them to keep them as happy and healthy as possible.

Keeping Up With Nutrition Trends

New research can show the roles of nutrients that were overlooked or unknown. A small breakthrough can have massive implications for dog health. When it was discovered that the vitamin C in fresh fruit prevents and treats scurvy, humans were able to undertake long sea voyages without scurvy's nasty symptoms. The same goes for dogs; a tiny new discovery can extend their lives and enhance their health.

Engaging With Dog Nutrition Communities

Communities can provide information and support through members who share your concerns. The joint experience and expertise of the community can lead you to discover new dog-safe ingredients, food-related health benefits, and harmful ingredients to avoid. Find dog nutrition communities with an internet search or start your own via social media.

Continuing Education for Optimal Pet Health

With all the new discoveries about dog nutrition and general pet health, staying on top of new developments will enable you to create the best environment for your beloved pet. Subscribe to the social media channels and websites of animal nutritionists and top dog food manufacturers to keep your dog's meals safe, balanced, and packed full of the right nutrients.

In the next chapter, we'll explore the guidelines, standards, and recommendations that will help you plan the healthiest meals.

7

Ensuring Nutritional Balance

The guidelines, recommendations, standards, and insights of groups committed to the best dog nutrition can help you tailor your dog food for the best results.

Understanding AAFCO Guidelines

The Association of American Feed Control Officials (AAFCO) established certain guidelines regarding pet nutrition. In this section, we'll look at the guidelines and how you can meet their standards in your home-cooked meals.

Key Nutrient Profiles for Dogs

The AAFCO nutrient profiles for dogs are guidelines to help you incorporate the minimum and maximum levels of essential nutrients dogs need during different life stages.

How to Meet AAFCO Standards in Homemade Meals

These are the minimum criteria for food to earn the AAFCO "complete and balanced" label;

- AAFCO suggests that adult dogs should have a diet consisting of 5.5% fats, 18% protein, and various vitamins and minerals.
- Puppies and pregnant dogs need 8.5% fats, 22.5% fats, and various vitamins and minerals.

Importance of Complete and Balanced Diets

Diets that meet the AAFCO guidelines contain the minimum nutrients a dog needs to maintain health. We've seen in the previous chapters that dogs can have different nutritional needs according to age and breed as well. Use the AAFCO nutrient profiles as a baseline and adapt your dog's diet according to its individual needs.

A complete and balanced diet ensures your dog can grow and thrive with optimal health and improved longevity.

WSAVA Global Nutrition Committee Insights

The World Small Animal Veterinary Association (WSAVA) researches and publishes guidelines regarding pet nutrition for veterinary teams and home pet owners.

Core Nutritional Recommendations

WSAVA's website has a handy chart listing the recommendations for daily calories according to dogs' weight (Calorie Ranges for an Average Healthy Adult Dog, n.d.). Keep in mind that the recommended calories are based on the statistics of average, healthy dogs and that you have to adjust according to your dog's age, activity level, breed, health conditions, and whether your dog is pregnant or lactating.

Tailoring Diets to Meet Global Standards

To align your dog food with WSAVA international standards, you should include vitamins, minerals, fats, proteins, and carbohydrates. The protein should be high-quality and include the essential amino acids a dog needs. The fats must be healthy fats that supply essential fatty acids, and the carbohydrates must be dog-friendly and not sourced from vegetables harmful to pets.

Balancing Homemade Meals

The ideal nutrient balance for the average dog contains 20–30% protein, 10–15% fat, and 40–50% carbohydrates. This balance varies according to your dog's needs. In this section, we'll briefly discuss how you can make sure your dog's diet stays balanced.

Using Supplements to Fill Nutritional Gaps

It can be difficult to supply all your dog's micronutrient needs (vitamins and minerals) through diet alone. Your veterinarian can examine your dog's diet and suggest any needed supplements. The ratios of the nutrients in the supplements are an important factor for their proper absorption, which is why working with a vet is the ideal option. Note that human supplements may contain ingredients that can damage a dog's health.

Regularly Assessing Your Dog's Health

Because allergies, sensitivities, deficiencies, and other conditions may pop up at any time, it is important to keep an eye on your dog's health. Symptoms such as lethargy, hair loss, loss of appetite, and frequent scratching may indicate that a diet adjustment is in order. Your local vet can help you reassess your dog's diet, and regular check-ups can catch any health and dietary issues early.

Adjusting Recipes for Compliance

Dog food recipes by nutrition experts are more likely to be WSAVA compliant. Recipes developed in conjunction with university veterinary programs and other veterinary resources are ideal.

You can also work with a veterinary nutritionist who is specifically trained to formulate diets that will be specific to your dog's individual requirements and taste.

8

Simple and Nutritious Everyday Meals

Tail-Wagging Turkey & Sweet Potato Stew

A hearty meal combining lean turkey and nutrient-rich sweet potatoes to support your dog's overall health.

Yield:	Time to Prepare:	Time to Cook:
6 cups	15 minutes	6 - 8 hours

Ingredients:

- 3 cups (1 ½ pounds) ground turkey
- 1 cup diced sweet potatoes
- 1 cup diced carrots
- 1 cup chopped green beans
- ½ cup brown rice
- 3 cups low-sodium chicken broth
- 1 tablespoon olive oil
- ½ teaspoon ground turmeric
- ½ teaspoon dried rosemary
- ¼ teaspoon ground flaxseed
- 1 crushed eggshell (for calcium)

Instructions:

1) Combine ground turkey, sweet potatoes, carrots, green beans, and brown rice in the slow cooker.
2) Pour in the low-sodium chicken broth.
3) Add olive oil, ground turmeric, dried rosemary, ground flaxseed, and the crushed eggshell.
4) Stir to mix all ingredients thoroughly.
5) Cover and cook on low for 6 - 8 hours.
6) Allow the stew to cool before serving.
7) Store leftovers in the refrigerator for up to 3 days.

Nutritional info per 1 Cup:
Calories: 200, Sodium: 48 mg, Dietary Fiber: 2.4 g, Fat: 8 g, Carbs: 16 g, Protein: 16 g

Barking Beef & Barley Delight

A savory blend of beef and barley, providing essential amino acids and fiber for your furry friend.

Yield:	Time to Prepare:	Time to Cook:
6 cups	15 minutes	6 - 8 hours

Ingredients:

3 cups (1 ½ pounds) lean ground beef

¾ cup pearl barley

¾ cup diced carrots

¾ cup chopped spinach

¾ cup diced zucchini

3 cups water

1 ½ tablespoons coconut oil

½ teaspoon dried parsley

½ teaspoon kelp powder (for iodine)

½ teaspoon ground eggshell (for calcium)

Instructions:

1) Combine ground beef, pearl barley, carrots, spinach, and zucchini in the slow cooker.
1) Add water, coconut oil, dried parsley, kelp powder, and ground eggshell.
2) Stir to mix all ingredients thoroughly.
3) Cover and cook on low for 6 - 8 hours.
4) Allow the mixture to cool before serving.
5) Store leftovers in the refrigerator for up to 3 days.

Nutritional info per 1 Cup:
Calories: 240, Sodium: 42 mg, Dietary Fiber: 2 g, Fat: 10 g, Carbs: 18 g, Protein: 18 g

Puppy Love Chicken & Rice Medley

A gentle and easily digestible meal, perfect for puppies and dogs with sensitive stomachs.

Yield:	Time to Prepare:	Time to Cook:
6 cups	10 minutes	6 - 8 hours

Ingredients:

- 3 cups (1 ½ pounds) boneless, skinless chicken breasts
- ¾ cup brown rice
- ¾ cup diced carrots
- ¾ cup peas
- ¾ cup diced apples (core removed)
- 3 cups water
- ¾ tablespoon fish oil (for omega-3 fatty acids)
- ½ teaspoon dried basil
- ½ teaspoon ground eggshell (for calcium)

Instructions:

1) Place chicken breasts, brown rice, carrots, peas, and apples into the slow cooker.
2) Pour in the water.
3) Add fish oil, dried basil, and ground eggshell.
4) Stir to combine all ingredients.
5) Cover and cook on low for 6 - 8 hours.
6) Once cooked, shred the chicken and mix thoroughly.
7) Allow the medley to cool before serving.
8) Store leftovers in the refrigerator for up to 3 days.

Nutritional Info per 1 Cup:
Calories: 180, Sodium: 32 mg, Dietary Fiber: 1.4 g, Fat: 6.2 g, Carbs: 14 g, Protein: 18 g

Furry Friend Fish & Potato Feast

A delightful combination of fish and potatoes, rich in omega-3 fatty acids for a healthy coat.

Yield:	Time to Prepare:	Time to Cook:
5 cups	10 minutes	4 - 6 hours

Ingredients:

2 ½ cups (1 ¼ pounds) boneless, skinless salmon fillets

1 cup diced potatoes

¾ cup chopped green beans

¾ cup diced carrots

¾ cup quinoa

3 cups water

1 tablespoon olive oil

½ teaspoon dried dill

½ teaspoon ground eggshell (for calcium

Instructions:

1) Place salmon fillets, potatoes, green beans, carrots, and quinoa into the slow cooker.
2) Add water, olive oil, dried dill, and ground eggshell.
3) Stir to combine all ingredients.
4) Cover and cook on low for 4 - 6 hours.
5) Once cooked, flake the salmon and mix thoroughly.
6) Allow the feast to cool before serving.
7) Store leftovers in the refrigerator for up to 2 days.

Nutritional info per 1 Cup:
Calories: 260, Sodium: 45 mg, Dietary Fiber: 2 g, Fat: 9 g, Carbs: 18 g, Protein: 23 g

Canine Comfort Lamb & Lentil Stew

A savory lamb and lentil stew, providing high-quality protein and fiber for sustained energy.

Yield:	Time to Prepare:	Time to Cook:
6 cups	15 minutes	6 - 8 hours

Ingredients:

- 3 cups (1 ½ pounds) lean ground lamb
- ¾ cup dried green lentils
- ¾ cup diced carrots
- ¾ cup chopped spinach
- ¾ cup diced sweet potatoes
- 3 cups low-sodium chicken broth
- 1 ½ tablespoons olive oil
- ½ teaspoon dried rosemary
- ½ teaspoon ground flaxseed (for omega-3s)
- ½ teaspoon kelp powder (for iodine)
- ½ teaspoon crushed eggshell (for calcium)

Instructions:

1) Combine ground lamb, green lentils, carrots, spinach, and sweet potatoes in the slow cooker.
2) Pour in the low-sodium chicken broth.
3) Add olive oil, dried rosemary, ground flaxseed, kelp powder, and crushed eggshell.
4) Stir well to combine all the ingredients.
5) Cover and cook on low for 6 - 8 hours, stirring occasionally if possible.
6) Once cooked, ensure the lentils are tender.
7) Allow the stew to cool slightly before serving.
8) Store leftovers in an airtight container in the refrigerator for up to 3 days.

Nutritional info per 1 Cup:
Calories: 250, Sodium: 56 mg, Dietary Fiber: 3 g, Fat: 11 g, Carbs: 16 g, Protein: 19 g

Wag-Worthy Chicken & Pumpkin Delight

A tasty, fiber-rich dish to support healthy digestion and a shiny coat.

Yield:	Time to Prepare:	Time to Cook:
6 cups	15 minutes	6 - 8 hours

Ingredients:

- 3 cups (1 ½ pounds) boneless, skinless chicken thighs
- 1 cup pumpkin puree (unsweetened)
- ¾ cup diced carrots
- ¾ cup chopped spinach
- ¾ cup brown rice
- 2 ½ cups low-sodium chicken broth
- 1 ½ tablespoons flaxseed oil
- ½ teaspoon dried oregano
- ½ crushed eggshell (for calcium)

Instructions:

1) Add chicken thighs, pumpkin puree, carrots, spinach, and brown rice to the slow cooker.
2) Pour in the chicken broth and add flaxseed oil, oregano, and crushed eggshell.
3) Stir well to combine all ingredients.
4) Cover and cook on low for 6 - 8 hours.
5) Shred the chicken and mix thoroughly once cooked.
6) Let the mixture cool before serving.
7) Store leftovers in the refrigerator for up to 3 days.

Nutritional info per 1 Cup:
Calories: 220, Sodium: 38 mg, Dietary Fiber: 2.5 g, Fat: 8.5 g, Carbs: 18.5 g, Protein: 19.5 g

Beefy Carrot & Spinach Super Stew

Packed with vitamins and minerals, this meal helps support strong muscles and a healthy immune system.

Yield:	Time to Prepare:	Time to Cook:
6 cups	15 minutes	6 - 8 hours

Ingredients:

- 3 cups (1 ½ pounds) lean ground beef
- 1 cup diced carrots
- ¾ cup chopped spinach
- ¾ cup diced sweet potatoes
- ¾ cup quinoa
- 2 ½ cups water
- 1 ½ tablespoons fish oil (rich in omega-3s)
- ½ teaspoon dried parsley
- ½ teaspoon ground eggshell (for calcium)

Instructions:

1) Place ground beef, carrots, spinach, sweet potatoes, and quinoa in the slow cooker.
2) Add water, fish oil, dried parsley, and ground eggshell.
3) Stir the mixture until well combined.
4) Cover and cook on low for 6 - 8 hours.
5) Stir again before serving and allow to cool.
6) Store leftovers in an airtight container in the refrigerator for up to 4 days.

Nutritional info per 1 Cup:
Calories: 240, Sodium: 42 mg, Dietary Fiber: 2 g, Fat: 10 g, Carbs: 15 g, Protein: 20 g

Puppy Pleaser Apple & Pork Medley

A sweet and savory blend that's great for dogs of all ages and provides a natural source of fiber.

Yield:	Time to Prepare:	Time to Cook:
6 cups	15 minutes	6 - 8 hours

Ingredients:

3 cups (1 ½ pounds) lean ground pork

1 cup diced apples (core removed)

¾ cup diced carrots

¾ cup peas

¾ cup brown rice

2 ½ cups low-sodium chicken broth

1 ½ tablespoons coconut oil

½ teaspoon ground ginger

½ teaspoon ground eggshell (for calcium)

Instructions:

1) Add ground pork, apples, carrots, peas, and brown rice to the slow cooker.
2) Pour in chicken broth and add coconut oil, ground ginger, and ground eggshell.
3) Stir well to combine all ingredients.
4) Cover and cook on low for 6 - 8 hours.
5) Once cooked, stir the mixture thoroughly and let it cool before serving.
6) Store leftovers in the refrigerator for up to 3 days.

Nutritional info per 1 Cup:
Calories: 208, Sodium: 50 mg, Dietary Fiber: 2.5 g, Fat: 8 g, Carbs: 18 g, Protein: 18 g

Happy Hound Beef & Green Bean Casserole

A protein-packed recipe with green beans for added fiber, perfect for active dogs.

Yield:	Time to Prepare:	Time to Cook:
6 cups	**15 minutes**	**6 - 8 hours**

Ingredients:

- 3 cups (1 ½ pounds) lean ground beef
- ¾ cup chopped green beans
- ¾ cup diced carrots
- ¾ cup brown rice
- 1 cup diced sweet potatoes
- 2 ½ cups water
- 1 tablespoon olive oil
- ½ teaspoon dried basil
- ½ teaspoon kelp powder (for iodine)

Instructions:

1) Combine ground beef, green beans, carrots, brown rice, and sweet potatoes in the slow cooker.
2) Add water, olive oil, dried basil, and kelp powder.
3) Mix well to combine all ingredients.
4) Cover and cook on low for 6 - 8 hours.
5) Stir and allow the casserole to cool before serving.
6) Store leftovers in the refrigerator for up to 4 days.

Nutritional info per 1 Cup:
Calories: 240, Sodium: 46 mg, Dietary Fiber: 2.8 g, Fat: 10 g, Carbs: 19 g, Protein: 20 g

Bow-Wow Beef & Blueberry Boost

A nutrient-dense recipe featuring antioxidant-rich blueberries for a healthy coat and immune system.

Yield:	Time to Prepare:	Time to Cook:
6 cups	15 minutes	6 - 8 hours

Ingredients:

- 3 cups (1 ½ pounds) lean ground beef
- ¾ cup fresh blueberries
- 1 cup diced butternut squash
- ¾ cup chopped kale
- ¾ cup quinoa
- 2 ½ cups water
- 1 ½ tablespoons flaxseed oil
- ½ teaspoon ground cinnamon
- ½ teaspoon ground eggshell (for calcium)

Instructions:

1) Add ground beef, blueberries, butternut squash, kale, and quinoa to the slow cooker.
2) Pour in water, then add flaxseed oil, ground cinnamon, and ground eggshell.
3) Stir to combine all ingredients thoroughly.
4) Cover and cook on low for 6 - 8 hours.
5) Once cooked, stir and let it cool before serving.
6) Store leftovers in the refrigerator for up to 3 days.

Nutritional info per 1 Cup:
Calories: 220, Sodium: 40 mg, Dietary Fiber: 3 g, Fat: 9 g, Carbs: 17 g, Protein: 19 g

Sweet Potato & Chicken Comfort Bowl

A gentle, easily digestible meal combining lean chicken and sweet potatoes for a soothing treat.

Yield:	Time to Prepare:	Time to Cook:
6 cups	10 minutes	6 - 8 hours

Ingredients:

- 3 cups (1 ½ pounds) boneless, skinless chicken breasts
- 1 cup diced sweet potatoes
- ¾ cup chopped spinach
- ¾ cup brown rice
- 2 ½ cups water
- 1 ½ tablespoons flaxseed oil
- ½ teaspoon ground turmeric
- ½ crushed eggshell (for calcium)

Instructions:

1) Add chicken, sweet potatoes, spinach, and brown rice to the slow cooker.
2) Pour in water, then add flaxseed oil, turmeric, and crushed eggshell.
3) Stir well to mix all ingredients.
4) Cover and cook on low for 6 - 8 hours.
5) Shred the chicken and mix thoroughly before serving.
6) Let it cool completely before feeding.
7) Store leftovers in the refrigerator for up to 3 days.

Nutritional info per 1 Cup:
Calories: 220, Sodium: 33 mg, Dietary Fiber: 2.5 g, Fat: 7.5 g, Carbs: 18 g, Protein: 20 g

Balanced Beef & Barley Blend

A fiber-rich and protein-packed recipe that supports healthy digestion and energy levels.

Yield:	Time to Prepare:	Time to Cook:
6 cups	15 minutes	6 - 8 hours

Ingredients:

- 3 cups (1 ½ pounds) ground beef
- ¾ cup pearl barley
- ¾ cup diced sweet potatoes
- ¾ cup chopped green beans
- 3 cups low-sodium beef broth
- 1 ½ tablespoons coconut oil
- ½ teaspoon dried parsley
- ½ crushed eggshell (for calcium)

Instructions:

1) Place beef, barley, sweet potatoes, and green beans into the slow cooker.
2) Add beef broth, coconut oil, parsley, and crushed eggshell.
3) Stir well to mix all ingredients.
4) Cover and cook on low for 6 - 8 hours.
5) Let it cool before serving.
6) Store leftovers in the refrigerator for up to 4 days.

Nutritional info per 1 Cup:
Calories: 260, Sodium: 42 mg, Dietary Fiber: 2.5 g, Fat: 12.5 g, Carbs: 18 g, Protein: 20 g

Doggy Dream Beef & Broccoli Dinner

A nutrient-packed recipe with lean beef and fiber-rich broccoli, ideal for dogs of all ages.

Yield:	Time to Prepare:	Time to Cook:
6 cups	15 minutes	6 - 8 hours

Ingredients:

3 cups (1 ½ pounds) lean ground beef

¾ cup chopped broccoli

¾ cup diced carrots

¾ cup quinoa

3 cups low-sodium beef broth

1 ½ tablespoons olive oil

½ teaspoon dried parsley

½ crushed eggshell (for calcium)

Instructions:

1) Combine beef, broccoli, carrots, and quinoa in the slow cooker.
2) Pour in beef broth, add olive oil, parsley, and crushed eggshell.
3) Stir thoroughly to mix all ingredients.
4) Cover and cook on low for 6 - 8 hours.
5) Allow the food to cool before serving.
6) Store leftovers in the refrigerator for up to 4 days.

Nutritional info per 1 Cup:
Calories: 240, Sodium: 42 mg, Dietary Fiber: 2 g, Fat: 11 g, Carbs: 15 g, Protein: 20 g

Chicken & Veggie Supreme

A well-rounded meal with lean chicken and a variety of veggies for a balanced diet.

Yield:	Time to Prepare:	Time to Cook:
6 cups	10 minutes	6 - 8 hours

Ingredients:

3 cups (1 ½ pounds) boneless, skinless chicken thighs

¾ cup chopped green beans

¾ cup diced carrots

¾ cup peas

¾ cup brown rice

3 cups low-sodium chicken broth

1 ½ tablespoons flaxseed oil

½ teaspoon ground turmeric

½ crushed eggshell (for calcium)

Instructions:

1) Add chicken, green beans, carrots, peas, and brown rice to the slow cooker.
2) Pour in chicken broth, then add flaxseed oil, turmeric, and eggshell.
3) Stir well to mix all ingredients.
4) Cover and cook on low for 6 - 8 hours.
5) Shred the chicken and mix thoroughly before serving.
6) Let it cool before feeding.
7) Store leftovers in an airtight container in the refrigerator for up to 3 days.

Nutritional info per 1 Cup:
Calories: 208, Sodium: 33 mg, Dietary Fiber: 1.5 g, Fat: 8.5 g, Carbs: 15 g, Protein: 18 g

Salmon & Spinach Omega Boost

A nourishing blend of salmon and spinach, rich in omega-3s to promote a healthy coat and skin.

Yield:	Time to Prepare:	Time to Cook:
6 cups	10 minutes	4-6 hours

Ingredients:

- 3 cups (1 ½ pounds) boneless, skinless salmon fillets
- ¾ cup chopped spinach
- ¾ cup diced potatoes
- ¾ cup brown rice
- 3 cups water
- 1 ½ tablespoons flaxseed oil
- ½ teaspoon dried dill
- ½ crushed eggshell (for calcium)

Instructions:

1) Add salmon, spinach, potatoes, and brown rice to the slow cooker.
2) Pour in water, then add flaxseed oil, dill, and crushed eggshell.
3) Stir thoroughly to combine all ingredients.
4) Cover and cook on low for 4-6 hours.
5) Flake the salmon and mix well before serving.
6) Let the food cool before feeding your dog.
7) Store leftovers in the refrigerator for up to 2 days.

Nutritional info per 1 Cup:
Calories: 220, Sodium: 38 mg, Dietary Fiber: 1.8 g, Fat: 10 g, Carbs: 15 g, Protein: 20 g

All-Dog Beef & Pumpkin Mash

A wholesome and easily digestible meal featuring lean beef and pumpkin, great for digestive health.

Yield:	Time to Prepare:	Time to Cook:
6 cups	10 minutes	6 - 8 hours

Ingredients:

3 cups (1 ½ pounds) ground beef

¾ cup pumpkin puree (unsweetened)

¾ cup diced green beans

¾ cup brown rice

3 cups water

1 ½ tablespoons olive oil

½ teaspoon dried thyme

½ crushed eggshell (for calcium)

Instructions:

1) Place beef, pumpkin, green beans, and brown rice into the slow cooker.
2) Add water, olive oil, thyme, and crushed eggshell.
3) Stir well to combine all ingredients.
4) Cover and cook on low for 6 - 8 hours.
5) Let the food cool before serving it to your dog.
6) Store leftovers in an airtight container in the refrigerator for up to 4 days.

Nutritional info per 1 Cup:
Calories: 225, Sodium: 38 mg, Dietary Fiber: 2.8 g, Fat: 10 g, Carbs: 16 g, Protein: 18 g

Beef & Apple Autumn Harvest

A hearty and flavorful mix of beef and apples, perfect for fall and great for overall health.

Yield:	Time to Prepare:	Time to Cook:
6 cups	10 minutes	6 - 8 hours

Ingredients:

3 cups (1 ½ pounds) ground beef

¾ cup diced apples (core removed)

¾ cup diced butternut squash

¾ cup quinoa

3 cups low-sodium beef broth

1 ½ tablespoons coconut oil

½ teaspoon ground cinnamon

½ crushed eggshell (for calcium)

Instructions:

1) Combine beef, apples, butternut squash, and quinoa in the slow cooker.
2) Pour in beef broth, add coconut oil, cinnamon, and crushed eggshell.
3) Stir well and cover to cook on low for 6 - 8 hours.
4) Let it cool before serving.
5) Store leftovers in the refrigerator for up to 4 days.

Nutritional info per 1 Cup:
Calories: 250, Sodium: 42 mg, Dietary Fiber: 2.8 g, Fat: 11 g, Carbs: 18 g, Protein: 20 g

Pork & Pear Harvest Mix

A savory and slightly sweet dish featuring pork and pears, perfect for picky eaters and dogs of all breeds.

Yield:	Time to Prepare:	Time to Cook:
6 cups	15 minutes	6 - 8 hours

Ingredients:

3 cups (1 ½ pounds) lean ground pork

¾ cup diced pears (core removed)

¾ cup diced butternut squash

¾ cup brown rice

3 cups water

1 ½ tablespoons olive oil

½ teaspoon ground ginger

½ crushed eggshell (for calcium)

Instructions:

1) Place pork, pears, butternut squash, and brown rice into the slow cooker.
2) Add water, olive oil, ginger, and crushed eggshell.
3) Stir to combine all ingredients well.
4) Cover and cook on low for 6 - 8 hours.
5) Mix thoroughly and allow it to cool before serving.
6) Store leftovers in the refrigerator for up to 3 days.

Nutritional Info per 1 Cup:
Calories: 225, Sodium: 28 mg, Dietary Fiber: 2.5 g, Fat: 9 g, Carbs: 15 g, Protein: 19 g

Salmon & Sweet Potato Delight

A hearty and nutritious recipe with salmon and sweet potatoes, providing omega-3 fatty acids for healthy skin and coat.

Yield:	Time to Prepare:	Time to Cook:
6 cups	10 minutes	4 - 6 hours

Ingredients:

- 3 cups (1 ½ pounds) boneless, skinless salmon fillets
- 1 cup diced sweet potatoes
- ¾ cup chopped spinach
- ¾ cup brown rice
- 3 cups water
- 1 ½ tablespoons flaxseed oil
- ½ teaspoon dried dill
- ½ crushed eggshell (for calcium)

Instructions:

1) Add salmon, sweet potatoes, spinach, and brown rice to the slow cooker.
2) Pour in water, then add flaxseed oil, dill, and crushed eggshell.
3) Stir thoroughly to combine.
4) Cover and cook on low for 4 - 6 hours.
5) Flake the salmon and mix well before serving.
6) Let it cool before feeding.
7) Store leftovers in an airtight container for up to 2 days.

Nutritional info per 1 Cup:
Calories: 240, Sodium: 38 mg, Dietary Fiber: 2 g, Fat: 10 g, Carbs: 16 g, Protein: 22 g

Pumpkin & Chicken Digestive Delight

A comforting blend of chicken and pumpkin, great for dogs with sensitive stomachs and digestive issues.

Yield:	Time to Prepare:	Time to Cook:
6 cups	15 minutes	6 - 8 hours

Ingredients:

- 3 cups (1 ½ pounds) boneless, skinless chicken breasts
- 1 cup pumpkin puree (unsweetened)
- ¾ cup diced carrots
- ¾ cup chopped green beans
- ¾ cup brown rice
- 3 cups low-sodium chicken broth
- 1 ½ tablespoons olive oil
- ½ teaspoon ground ginger
- ½ crushed eggshell (for calcium)

Instructions:

1) Add chicken, pumpkin, carrots, green beans, and brown rice to the slow cooker.
2) Pour in chicken broth, then add olive oil, ground ginger, and crushed eggshell.
3) Stir thoroughly to mix all ingredients.
4) Cover and cook on low for 6 - 8 hours.
5) Shred the chicken and stir well before serving.
6) Allow the food to cool completely before feeding your dog.
7) Store leftovers in an airtight container in the refrigerator for up to 3 days.

Nutritional info per 1 Cup:
Calories: 200, Sodium: 32 mg, Dietary Fiber: 2.5 g, Fat: 7.5 g, Carbs: 15 g, Protein: 19 g

9

Quick-Prep Options for Busy Days

Paws-itively Perfect Chicken & Brown Rice Bowl

A comforting and easily digestible meal packed with lean chicken and whole grains.

Yield:	Time to Prepare:	Time to Cook:
6 cups	10 minutes	6 - 8 hours

Ingredients:

3 cups (1 ½ pounds) boneless, skinless chicken breasts

¾ cup brown rice

¾ cup diced carrots

¾ cup peas

3 cups low-sodium chicken broth

1 ½ tablespoons olive oil

½ teaspoon dried thyme

½ teaspoon ground flaxseed

½ crushed eggshell (for calcium)

Instructions:

1) Combine chicken breasts, brown rice, carrots, and peas in the slow cooker.
2) Add chicken broth, olive oil, dried thyme, flaxseed, and eggshell.
3) Stir well and cover to cook on low for 6 - 8 hours.
4) Shred the chicken and mix thoroughly before serving.
5) Let it cool before feeding your dog.
6) Store leftovers in the refrigerator for up to 3 days.

Nutritional info per 1 Cup:
Calories: 183, Sodium: 38 mg, Dietary Fiber: 1.5 g, Fat: 6.6 g, Carbs: 15 g, Protein: 16.6 g

Tail-Wagging Turkey & Veggie Medley

A lean and nutritious turkey recipe with a medley of fresh veggies for a balanced meal.

Yield:	Time to Prepare:	Time to Cook:
6 cups	**15 minutes**	**6 - 8 hours**

Ingredients:

- 3 cups (1 ½ pounds) ground turkey
- ¾ cup diced zucchini
- ¾ cup diced carrots
- ¾ cup green beans
- ¾ cup quinoa
- 3 cups water
- 1 ½ tablespoons flaxseed oil
- ½ teaspoon dried oregano
- ½ crushed eggshell (for calcium)

Instructions:

1) Add ground turkey, zucchini, carrots, green beans, and quinoa to the slow cooker.
2) Pour in water, flaxseed oil, dried oregano, and eggshell.
3) Stir to combine all ingredients well.
4) Cover and cook on low for 6 - 8 hours.
5) Mix thoroughly before serving.
6) Store in an airtight container for up to 4 days in the refrigerator.

Nutritional info per 1 Cup:
Calories: 200, Sodium: 38 mg, Dietary Fiber: 2.1 g, Fat: 8.3 g, Carbs: 15 g, Protein: 18.3 g

Woof-Worthy Beef & Barley Bliss

Rich in protein and fiber, this beef and barley stew supports healthy digestion and muscle maintenance.

Yield:	Time to Prepare:	Time to Cook:
6 cups	15 minutes	6 - 8 hours

Ingredients:

3 cups (1 ½ pounds) ground beef

¾ cup pearl barley

¾ cup diced sweet potatoes

¾ cup chopped spinach

3 cups low-sodium beef broth

1 tablespoon coconut oil

½ teaspoon dried basil

½ crushed eggshell (for calcium)

Instructions:

1) Combine beef, barley, sweet potatoes, and spinach in the slow cooker.
2) Add beef broth, coconut oil, dried basil, and eggshell.
3) Stir well and cook on low for 6 - 8 hours.
4) Let the stew cool before serving it to your dog.
5) Store any leftovers in the refrigerator for up to 4 days.

Nutritional Info per 1 Cup:
Calories: 240, Sodium: 46 mg, Dietary Fiber: 2.5 g, Fat: 11 g, Carbs: 18 g, Protein: 20 g

Speedy Salmon & Potato Power-Up

A fast-cooking meal featuring salmon and potatoes, providing a boost of omega-3s for a shiny coat.

Yield:	Time to Prepare:	Time to Cook:
6 cups	10 minutes	4 - 6 hours

Ingredients:

- 3 cups (1 ½ pounds) boneless, skinless salmon fillets
- 1 cup diced potatoes
- ¾ cup chopped green beans
- ¾ cup quinoa
- 3 cups water
- 1 ½ tablespoons olive oil
- ½ teaspoon dried dill
- ½ crushed eggshell (for calcium)

Instructions:

1) Place salmon, potatoes, green beans, and quinoa in the slow cooker.
2) Pour in water, add olive oil, dried dill, and eggshell.
3) Mix ingredients and cover to cook on low for 4-6 hours.
4) Flake the salmon and stir before serving.
5) Store leftovers in the fridge for up to 2 days.

Nutritional Info per 1 Cup:
Calories: 240, Sodium: 33 mg, Dietary Fiber: 1.8 g, Fat: 10 g, Carbs: 15 g, Protein: 20 g

Fast & Fluffy Turkey & Pumpkin Chow

A tummy-friendly dish combining turkey and pumpkin for quick, easy prep.

Yield:	Time to Prepare:	Time to Cook:
6 cups	10 minutes	6 - 8 hours

Ingredients:

3 cups (1 ½ pounds) ground turkey

¾ cup pumpkin puree

¾ cup diced carrots

¾ cup peas

3 cups water

1 ½ tablespoons flaxseed oil

½ teaspoon dried parsley

½ crushed eggshell (for calcium)

Instructions:

1) Add turkey, pumpkin, carrots, and peas to the slow cooker.
2) Pour in water, then add flaxseed oil, parsley, and eggshell.
3) Stir well and cook on low for 6 - 8 hours.
4) Let it cool before serving.
5) Store in the refrigerator for up to 3 days.

Nutritional info per 1 Cup:
Calories: 200, Sodium: 25 mg, Dietary Fiber: 2.5 g, Fat: 8.3 g, Carbs: 15 g, Protein: 18.3 g

Quick Beef & Sweet Pea Mash

A hearty and delicious meal ready in no time, perfect for busy pet parents.

Yield:	Time to Prepare:	Time to Cook:
6 cups	15 minutes	6 - 8 hours

Ingredients:

3 cups (1 ½ pounds) ground beef

¾ cup sweet peas

¾ cup diced butternut squash

¾ cup quinoa

3 cups water

1 ½ tablespoons coconut oil

½ teaspoon ground turmeric

½ crushed eggshell (for calcium)

Instructions:

1) Place beef, peas, butternut squash, and quinoa in the slow cooker.
2) Add water, coconut oil, turmeric, and eggshell.
3) Stir well and cook on low for 6 - 8 hours.
4) Let it cool before serving.
5) Store leftovers in the refrigerator for up to 4 days.

Nutritional info per 1 Cup:
Calories: 230, Sodium: 28 mg, Dietary Fiber: 2.1 g, Fat: 10 g, Carbs: 15 g, Protein: 19 g

Chicken & Spinach Express Delight

A quick and nutritious chicken recipe with the added benefits of leafy greens for strong bones.

Yield:	Time to Prepare:	Time to Cook:
6 cups	10 minutes	6 - 8 hours

Ingredients:

3 cups (1 ½ pounds) boneless, skinless chicken thighs

¾ cup chopped spinach

¾ cup diced carrots

¾ cup brown rice

3 cups low-sodium chicken broth

1 ½ tablespoons flaxseed oil

½ teaspoon ground turmeric

½ crushed eggshell (for calcium)

Instructions:

1) Add chicken, spinach, carrots, and brown rice to the slow cooker.
2) Pour in chicken broth and add flaxseed oil, turmeric, and ground eggshell.
3) Stir the mixture and cover to cook on low for 6 - 8 hours.
4) Shred the chicken and mix well before serving.
5) Let it cool before feeding your dog.
6) Store leftovers in the refrigerator for up to 3 days.

Nutritional info per 1 Cup:
Calories: 210, Sodium: 33 mg, Dietary Fiber: 1.8 g, Fat: 8 g, Carbs: 15 g, Protein: 18 g

Speedy Pork & Apple Mash-Up

A delicious pork and apple combo that offers a natural source of vitamins and fiber.

Yield:	Time to Prepare:	Time to Cook:
6 cups	15 minutes	6 - 8 hours

Ingredients:

- 3 cups (1 ½ pounds) lean ground pork
- ¾ cup diced apples (core removed)
- ¾ cup diced sweet potatoes
- ¾ cup quinoa
- 3 cups water
- 1 tablespoon coconut oil
- ½ teaspoon ground cinnamon
- ½ crushed eggshell (for calcium)

Instructions:

1) Combine pork, apples, sweet potatoes, and quinoa in the slow cooker.
2) Pour in water, add coconut oil, cinnamon, and crushed eggshell.
3) Stir well to mix all ingredients.
4) Cover and cook on low for 6 - 8 hours.
5) Stir thoroughly and let it cool before serving.
6) Store any leftovers in the refrigerator for up to 3 days.

Nutritional info per 1 Cup:
Calories: 210, Sodium: 28 mg, Dietary Fiber: 2.2 g, Fat: 9 g, Carbs: 15 g, Protein: 18 g

Salmon & Blueberry Booster Bowl

A quick and antioxidant-rich meal with salmon and blueberries to support immune health.

Yield:	Time to Prepare:	Time to Cook:
6 cups	10 minutes	4 - 6 hours

Ingredients:

- 3 cups (1 ½ pounds) boneless, skinless salmon fillets
- ¾ cup fresh blueberries
- ¾ cup diced carrots
- ¾ cup brown rice
- 3 cups water
- 1 ½ tablespoons olive oil
- ½ teaspoon dried dill
- ½ crushed eggshell (for calcium)

Instructions:

1) Add salmon, blueberries, carrots, and brown rice to the slow cooker.
2) Pour in water, then add olive oil, dill, and ground eggshell.
3) Stir to combine the ingredients well.
4) Cover and cook on low for 4 - 6 hours.
5) Flake the salmon and mix thoroughly before serving.
6) Let it cool before feeding your dog.
7) Store leftovers in an airtight container for up to 2 days.

Nutritional Info per 1 Cup:
Calories: 240, Sodium: 30 mg, Dietary Fiber: 1.8 g, Fat: 10 g, Carbs: 15 g, Protein: 20 g

Turbo Turkey & Butternut Squash Chow

A hearty and flavorful meal featuring lean turkey and fiber-rich butternut squash.

Yield:	Time to Prepare:	Time to Cook:
6 cups	15 minutes	6 - 8 hours

Ingredients:

- 3 cups (1 ½ pounds) ground turkey
- 1 cup diced butternut squash
- ¾ cup chopped kale
- ¾ cup diced apples (core removed)
- 3 cups low-sodium chicken broth
- 1 ½ tablespoons flaxseed oil
- ½ teaspoon ground ginger
- ½ tablespoon ground chia seeds (for calcium)

Instructions:

1) Add turkey, butternut squash, kale, and apples to the slow cooker.
2) Pour in chicken broth, then add flaxseed oil, ground ginger, and ground chia seeds.
3) Stir the mixture thoroughly.
4) Cover and cook on low for 6 - 8 hours.
5) Mix well before serving and allow it to cool completely.
6) Store leftovers in the refrigerator for up to 3 days.

Nutritional info per 1 Cup:
Calories: 215, Sodium: 38 mg, Dietary Fiber: 2.4 g, Fat: 9 g, Carbs: 16 g, Protein: 18 g

Pork & Pumpkin Perfect Stew

A savory and sweet pork and pumpkin dish that's great for digestion and picky eaters.

Yield:	Time to Prepare:	Time to Cook:
6 cups	15 minutes	6 - 8 hours

Ingredients:

3 cups (1 ½ pounds) lean ground pork

1 cup pumpkin puree (unsweetened)

¾ cup diced carrots

¾ cup brown rice

3 cups water

1 ½ tablespoons olive oil

½ teaspoon ground ginger

½ tablespoon ground sesame seeds (for calcium)

Instructions:

1) Add pork, pumpkin, carrots, and brown rice to the slow cooker.
2) Pour in water, then add olive oil, ground ginger, and ground sesame seeds.
3) Stir thoroughly to mix.
4) Cover and cook on low for 6 - 8 hours.
5) Let it cool completely before feeding your dog.
6) Store leftovers in an airtight container for up to 3 days.

Nutritional info per 1 Cup:
Calories: 225, Sodium: 30 mg, Dietary Fiber: 2.5 g, Fat: 10 g, Carbs: 15 g, Protein: 19 g

Express Beef & Spinach Stew

A quick and hearty meal featuring lean beef and iron-rich spinach.

Yield:	Time to Prepare:	Time to Cook:
6 cups	10 minutes	6 - 8 hours

Ingredients:

3 cups (1 ½ pounds) lean ground beef

¾ cup chopped spinach

¾ cup diced carrots

¾ cup quinoa

3 cups low-sodium beef broth

1 ½ tablespoons flaxseed oil

½ teaspoon dried basil

½ tablespoon crushed eggshell powder (for calcium)

Instructions:

1) Combine beef, spinach, carrots, and quinoa in the slow cooker.
2) Add beef broth, flaxseed oil, basil, and crushed eggshell powder.
3) Stir well and cover to cook on low for 6 - 8 hours.
4) Mix thoroughly before serving and let it cool completely.
5) Store leftovers in the refrigerator for up to 4 days.

Nutritional info per 1 Cup:
Calories: 233, Sodium: 38 mg, Dietary Fiber: 2 g, Fat: 11 g, Carbs: 15 g, Protein: 19 g

Quick Cod & Pumpkin Stew

A light and nutrient-dense dish featuring cod and pumpkin, perfect for dogs needing a gentle meal.

Yield:	Time to Prepare:	Time to Cook:
6 cups	10 minutes	4 - 6 hours

Ingredients:

3 cups (1 ½ pounds) boneless cod fillets

1 cup pumpkin puree (unsweetened)

¾ cup diced zucchini

¾ cup brown rice

3 cups water

1 ½ tablespoons olive oil

½ teaspoon dried dill

½ tablespoon ground chia seeds (for calcium)

Instructions:

1) Place cod, pumpkin, zucchini, and brown rice in the slow cooker.
2) Add water, olive oil, dill, and ground chia seeds.
3) Stir well to mix all ingredients.
4) Cover and cook on low for 4 - 6 hours.
5) Flake the cod and mix thoroughly before serving.
6) Let it cool completely before feeding.
7) Store leftovers in the refrigerator for up to 2 days.

Nutritional info per 1 Cup:
Calories: 210, Sodium: 28 mg, Dietary Fiber: 1.5 g, Fat: 8 g, Carbs: 14 g, Protein: 17 g

Fast Lamb & Green Bean Casserole

A tasty and quick-prep lamb recipe with green beans for added fiber and vitamins.

Yield:	Time to Prepare:	Time to Cook:
6 cups	15 minutes	6 - 8 hours

Ingredients:

- 3 cups (1 ½ pounds) ground lamb
- ¾ cup chopped green beans
- ¾ cup diced carrots
- ¾ cup quinoa
- 3 cups low-sodium chicken broth
- 1 ½ tablespoons coconut oil
- ½ teaspoon dried rosemary
- ½ tablespoon ground sunflower seeds (for calcium)

Instructions:

1) Add lamb, green beans, carrots, and quinoa to the slow cooker.
2) Pour in chicken broth, then add coconut oil, rosemary, and ground sunflower seeds.
3) Stir thoroughly to mix all ingredients.
4) Cover and cook on low for 6 - 8 hours.
5) Mix well before serving and allow it to cool.
6) Store leftovers in the refrigerator for up to 3 days.

Nutritional info per 1 Cup:
Calories: 242, Sodium: 36 mg, Dietary Fiber: 2 g, Fat: 11 g, Carbs: 15 g, Protein: 18 g

Salmon & Sweet Potato Delight

A hearty and nutritious recipe featuring salmon and sweet potatoes, rich in omega-3 fatty acids for skin and coat health.

Yield:	Time to Prepare:	Time to Cook:
6 cups	10 minutes	4 - 6 hours

Ingredients:

3 cups (1 ½ pounds) boneless, skinless salmon fillets

1 cup diced sweet potatoes

¾ cup chopped kale

¾ cup quinoa

3 cups water

1 ½ tablespoons flaxseed oil

½ teaspoon dried dill

½ tablespoon ground sesame seeds (for calcium)

Instructions:

1) Place salmon, sweet potatoes, kale, and quinoa into the slow cooker.
2) Add water, flaxseed oil, dill, and ground sesame seeds.
3) Stir thoroughly to mix all ingredients.
4) Cover and cook on low for 4 - 6 hours.
5) Flake the salmon and stir well before serving.
6) Let the food cool before feeding your dog. Store leftovers in an airtight container for up to 2 days.

Nutritional info per 1 Cup:
Calories: 240, Sodium: 30 mg, Dietary Fiber: 2 g, Fat: 10 g, Carbs: 14 g, Protein: 20 g

Rapid Chicken & Kale Dinner

A nutritious chicken and kale meal that cooks quickly, offering a boost of vitamins and minerals.

Yield:	Time to Prepare:	Time to Cook:
6 cups	10 minutes	6 - 8 hours

Ingredients:

- 3 cups (1 ½ pounds) boneless, skinless chicken thighs
- ¾ cup chopped kale
- ¾ cup diced carrots
- ¾ cup brown rice
- 3 cups low-sodium chicken broth
- 1 ½ tablespoons olive oil
- ½ teaspoon dried thyme
- ½ tablespoon powdered eggshell (for calcium)

Instructions:

1) Combine chicken, kale, carrots, and brown rice in the slow cooker.
2) Pour in chicken broth, add olive oil, thyme, and powdered eggshell.
3) Stir to mix all ingredients well.
4) Cover and cook on low for 6 - 8 hours.
5) Shred the chicken and stir well before serving.
6) Allow the food to cool before feeding your dog.
7) Store leftovers in the refrigerator for up to 3 days.

Nutritional info per 1 Cup:
Calories: 208, Sodium: 28 mg, Dietary Fiber: 2.5 g, Fat: 8 g, Carbs: 14 g, Protein: 18 g

Universal Turkey & Brown Rice Delight

A versatile, balanced meal featuring lean turkey and brown rice, perfect for dogs of all sizes.

Yield:	Time to Prepare:	Time to Cook:
6 cups	15 minutes	6 - 8 hours

Ingredients:

- 3 cups (1 ½ pounds) ground turkey
- ¾ cup brown rice
- ¾ cup diced carrots
- ¾ cup chopped spinach
- 3 cups low-sodium chicken broth
- 1 ½ tablespoons flaxseed oil
- ½ teaspoon dried oregano
- ½ tablespoon ground chia seeds (for calcium)

Instructions:

1) Add turkey, brown rice, carrots, and spinach to the slow cooker.
2) Pour in chicken broth, then add flaxseed oil, oregano, and ground chia seeds.
3) Stir to combine all ingredients.
4) Cover and cook on low for 6 - 8 hours.
5) Mix thoroughly and allow it to cool before serving.
6) Store leftovers in an airtight container in the refrigerator for up to 3 days.

Nutritional info per 1 Cup:
Calories: 210, Sodium: 30 mg, Dietary Fiber: 2.5 g, Fat: 8 g, Carbs: 16 g, Protein: 18 g

Tail-Wag Turkey & Blueberry Treat

A delicious blend of turkey and antioxidant-rich blueberries for a boost to your dog's immune system.

Yield:	Time to Prepare:	Time to Cook:
6 cups	10 minutes	6 - 8 hours

Ingredients:

3 cups (1 ½ pounds) ground turkey

¾ cup fresh blueberries

¾ cup diced zucchini

¾ cup quinoa

3 cups low-sodium chicken broth

1 ½ tablespoons flaxseed oil

½ teaspoon dried rosemary

½ tablespoon bone meal powder (for calcium)

Instructions:

1) Combine turkey, blueberries, zucchini, and quinoa in the slow cooker.
2) Pour in chicken broth, add flaxseed oil, rosemary, and bone meal powder.
3) Stir thoroughly and cover to cook on low for 6 - 8 hours.
4) Let the mixture cool completely before serving.
5) Store any leftovers in an airtight container in the refrigerator for up to 3 days.

Nutritional info per 1 Cup:
Calories: 215, Sodium: 32 mg, Dietary Fiber: 2 g, Fat: 9 g, Carbs: 15 g, Protein: 18 g Quickie Beef & Broccoli Blend

Woof-Worthy Beef & Barley Bliss

A protein-packed and fiber-rich meal, perfect for an energy boost on busy days.

Yield:	Time to Prepare:	Time to Cook:
6 cups	10 minutes	6 - 8 hours

Ingredients:

3 cups (1 ½ pounds) ground beef

¾ cup chopped broccoli

¾ cup diced sweet potatoes

¾ cup quinoa

3 cups water

1 ½ tablespoons coconut oil

½ teaspoon dried parsley

½ tablespoon powdered eggshell (for calcium)

Instructions:

1) Place beef, broccoli, sweet potatoes, and quinoa into the slow cooker.
2) Add water, coconut oil, parsley, and powdered eggshell.
3) Stir the ingredients well and cover to cook on low for 6 - 8 hours.
4) Mix thoroughly before serving and allow the food to cool.
5) Store leftovers in an airtight container in the refrigerator for up to 4 days.

Nutritional info per 1 Cup:
Calories: 230, Sodium: 30 mg, Dietary Fiber: 2.2 g, Fat: 10 g, Carbs: 14 g, Protein: 19 g

Speedy Pork & Pear Mash-Up

A delightful mix of lean pork and pears, offering a sweet and savory blend dogs love.

Yield:	Time to Prepare:	Time to Cook:
6 cups	10 minutes	4 -6 hours

Ingredients:

3 cups (1 ½ pounds) lean ground pork

¾ cup diced pears (core removed)

¾ cup diced carrots

¾ cup brown rice

3 cups low-sodium chicken broth

1 ½ tablespoons olive oil

½ teaspoon ground cinnamon

½ tablespoon ground sunflower seeds (for calcium)

Instructions:

1) Add pork, pears, carrots, and brown rice to the slow cooker.
2) Pour in chicken broth, then add olive oil, ground cinnamon, and ground sunflower seeds.
3) Stir thoroughly and cover to cook on low for 4 -6 hours.
4) Let it cool before serving.
5) Store leftovers in an airtight container in the refrigerator for up to 3 days.

Nutritional info per 1 Cup:
Calories: 225, Sodium: 35 mg, Dietary Fiber: 2.5 g, Fat: 9 g, Carbs: 15 g, Protein: 19 g

10

Versatile Recipes for All Dogs

All-Pup Lamb & Sweet Potato Stew

A balanced lamb and sweet potato dish suitable for dogs of all ages and breeds.

Yield:	Time to Prepare:	Time to Cook:
6 cups	15 minutes	6 - 8 hours

Ingredients:

3 cups (1 ½ pounds) lean ground lamb

1 cup diced sweet potatoes

¾ cup chopped kale

¾ cup quinoa

3 cups water

1 ½ tablespoons coconut oil

½ teaspoon dried rosemary

½ tablespoon bone meal powder (for calcium)

Instructions:

1) Place lamb, sweet potatoes, kale, and quinoa in the slow cooker.
2) Add water, coconut oil, rosemary, and bone meal powder.
3) Stir the mixture thoroughly.
4) Cover and cook on low for 6 - 8 hours.
5) Mix well and let it cool before serving.
6) Store leftovers in the refrigerator for up to 3 days.

Nutritional info per 1 Cup:
Calories: 225, Sodium: 36 mg, Dietary Fiber: 2.8 g, Fat: 10 g, Carbs: 15 g, Protein: 19 g

Universal Beef & Barley Chow

A hearty and filling recipe that suits dogs of all sizes, providing energy and muscle support.

Yield:	Time to Prepare:	Time to Cook:
6 cups	15 minutes	6 - 8 hours

Ingredients:

3 cups (1 ½ pounds) ground beef

¾ cup pearl barley

¾ cup diced carrots

¾ cup diced zucchini

3 cups low-sodium beef broth

1 ½ tablespoons olive oil

½ teaspoon dried parsley

½ tablespoon ground eggshell (for calcium)

Instructions:

1) Combine beef, barley, carrots, and zucchini in the slow cooker.
2) Pour in beef broth, add olive oil, parsley, and ground eggshell.
3) Stir well and cover to cook on low for 6 - 8 hours.
4) Let it cool before serving it to your dog.
5) Store leftovers in the refrigerator for up to 4 days.

Nutritional Info per 1 Cup:
Calories: 250, Sodium: 40 mg, Dietary Fiber: 2.5 g, Fat: 11 g, Carbs: 18 g, Protein: 20 g

Mighty Meat & Veggie Mix

A versatile, nutrient-dense mix of meat and vegetables, great for any dog's daily diet.

Yield:	Time to Prepare:	Time to Cook:
6 cups	15 minutes	6 - 8 hours

Ingredients:

- 3 cups (1 ½ pounds) ground beef
- ¾ cup diced carrots
- ¾ cup chopped spinach
- ¾ cup diced zucchini
- ¾ cup quinoa
- 3 cups water
- 1 ½ tablespoons coconut oil
- ½ teaspoon dried oregano
- ½ tablespoon crushed oyster shell powder (for calcium)

Instructions:

1) Place beef, carrots, spinach, zucchini, and quinoa in the slow cooker.
2) Add water, coconut oil, oregano, and crushed oyster shell powder.
3) Stir to mix all ingredients well.
4) Cover and cook on low for 6 - 8 hours.
5) Mix thoroughly and let it cool before feeding.
6) Store leftovers in an airtight container in the refrigerator for up to 3 days.

Nutritional info per 1 Cup:
Calories: 250, Sodium: 42 mg, Dietary Fiber: 2.6 g, Fat: 10 g, Carbs: 18 g, Protein: 20 g

Happy Paws Chicken & Oat Stew

A soothing and nourishing chicken and oat recipe, great for dogs with sensitive tummies.

Yield:	Time to Prepare:	Time to Cook:
6 cups	10 minutes	6 - 8 hours

Ingredients:

- 3 cups (1 ½ pounds) boneless, skinless chicken thighs
- ¾ cup rolled oats
- ¾ cup diced apples (core removed)
- ¾ cup chopped kale
- 3 cups low-sodium chicken broth
- 1 ½ tablespoons olive oil
- ½ teaspoon ground cinnamon
- ½ tablespoon ground chia seeds (for calcium)

Instructions:

1) Add chicken, oats, apples, and kale to the slow cooker.
2) Pour in chicken broth, olive oil, and cinnamon. Add ground chia seeds.
3) Stir the mixture thoroughly.
4) Cover and cook on low for 6 - 8 hours.
5) Shred the chicken and stir well before serving.
6) Let it cool completely before feeding.
7) Store leftovers in the refrigerator for up to 3 days.

Nutritional info per 1 Cup:
Calories: 220, Sodium: 32 mg, Dietary Fiber: 2.8 g, Fat: 8.6 g, Carbs: 16 g, Protein: 18 g

Pooch Perfect Turkey & Spinach Stew

A nutrient-rich stew with lean turkey and spinach, offering a well-rounded meal for any dog.

Yield:	Time to Prepare:	Time to Cook:
6 cups	15 minutes	6 - 8 hours

Ingredients:

- 3 cups (1 ½ pounds) ground turkey
- ¾ cup chopped spinach
- ¾ cup diced carrots
- ¾ cup diced sweet potatoes
- ¾ cup quinoa
- 3 cups low-sodium chicken broth
- 1 ½ tablespoons flaxseed oil
- ½ teaspoon dried basil
- ½ tablespoon ground sesame seeds (for calcium)

Instructions:

1) Combine turkey, spinach, carrots, sweet potatoes, and quinoa in the slow cooker.
2) Pour in chicken broth, add flaxseed oil, basil, and ground sesame seeds.
3) Stir well to mix all ingredients.
4) Cover and cook on low for 6 - 8 hours.
5) Mix thoroughly and allow it to cool before serving.
6) Store leftovers in the refrigerator for up to 3 days.

Nutritional info per 1 Cup:
Calories: 210, Sodium: 36 mg, Dietary Fiber: 2.4 g, Fat: 8 g, Carbs: 16 g, Protein: 18 g

Salmon & Sweet Pea Power Bowl

A nutrient-dense recipe with salmon and peas, providing a good source of omega-3s for a shiny coat.

Yield:	Time to Prepare:	Time to Cook:
6 cups	10 minutes	4 - 6 hours

Ingredients:

3 cups (1 ½ pounds) boneless, skinless salmon fillets

¾ cup sweet peas

1 cup diced potatoes

¾ cup quinoa

3 cups water

1 ½ tablespoons olive oil

½ teaspoon dried dill

½ tablespoon ground dried shrimp shells (for calcium)

Instructions:

1) Place salmon, sweet peas, potatoes, and quinoa into the slow cooker.
2) Add water, olive oil, dill, and ground dried shrimp shells.
3) Stir well and cover to cook on low for 4 - 6 hours.
4) Flake the salmon and mix thoroughly before serving.
5) Let the food cool before feeding your dog.
6) Store leftovers in the refrigerator for up to 2 days.

Nutritional info per 1 Cup:
Calories: 240, Sodium: 36 mg, Dietary Fiber: 1.9 g, Fat: 10 g, Carbs: 15 g, Protein: 20 g

Balanced Beef & Apple Supreme

A well-rounded recipe combining lean beef and apples, providing a tasty and nutritious meal for any dog.

Yield:	Time to Prepare:	Time to Cook:
6 cups	15 minutes	6 - 8 hours

Ingredients:

- 3 cups (1 ½ pounds) lean ground beef
- ¾ cup diced apples (core removed)
- ¾ cup diced carrots
- ¾ cup chopped spinach
- ¾ cup brown rice
- 3 cups low-sodium beef broth
- 1 ½ tablespoons coconut oil
- ½ teaspoon ground cinnamon
- ½ tablespoon ground sardine bones (for calcium)

Instructions:

1) Add beef, apples, carrots, spinach, and brown rice to the slow cooker.
2) Pour in beef broth, then add coconut oil, cinnamon, and ground sardine bones.
3) Stir thoroughly to mix all ingredients.
4) Cover and cook on low for 6 - 8 hours.
5) Mix well before serving and allow it to cool completely.
6) Store leftovers in the refrigerator for up to 3 days.

Nutritional info per 1 Cup:
Calories: 240, Sodium: 40 mg, Dietary Fiber: 2.3 g, Fat: 10 g, Carbs: 15 g, Protein: 20 g

Ultimate Chicken & Green Bean Chowder

A versatile and hearty chowder made with chicken and green beans, suitable for dogs of all breeds.

Yield:	Time to Prepare:	Time to Cook:
6 cups	15 minutes	6 - 8 hours

Ingredients:

- 3 cups (1 ½ pounds) boneless, skinless chicken thighs
- ¾ cup chopped green beans
- ¾ cup diced carrots
- ¾ cup barley
- 3 cups low-sodium chicken broth
- 1 ½ tablespoons olive oil
- ½ teaspoon dried parsley
- ½ tablespoon ground dried seaweed (for calcium)

Instructions:

1) Place chicken, green beans, carrots, and barley into the slow cooker.
2) Add chicken broth, olive oil, parsley, and ground dried seaweed.
3) Stir well and cover to cook on low for 6 - 8 hours.
4) Shred the chicken and mix thoroughly before serving.
5) Let the food cool completely before feeding.
6) Store leftovers in the refrigerator for up to 4 days.

Nutritional info per 1 Cup:
Calories: 210, Sodium: 35 mg, Dietary Fiber: 2.2 g, Fat: 9 g, Carbs: 15 g, Protein: 18 g

Mighty Meal Lamb & Lentil Mix

A hearty lamb and lentil recipe, perfect for dogs needing a protein boost and sustained energy.

Yield:	Time to Prepare:	Time to Cook:
6 cups	20 minutes	6 - 8 hours

Ingredients:

- 3 cups (1 ½ pounds) lean ground lamb
- ¾ cup dried lentils
- ¾ cup diced sweet potatoes
- ¾ cup chopped kale
- 3 cups low-sodium chicken broth
- 1 ½ tablespoons olive oil
- ½ teaspoon dried rosemary
- ½ tablespoon crushed coral calcium (for calcium)

Instructions:

1) Combine lamb, lentils, sweet potatoes, and kale in the slow cooker.
2) Add chicken broth, olive oil, rosemary, and crushed coral calcium.
3) Stir the mixture well.
4) Cover and cook on low for 6 - 8 hours.
5) Stir again before serving and allow it to cool completely.
6) Store leftovers in the refrigerator for up to 3 days.

Nutritional info per 1 Cup:
Calories: 230, Sodium: 40 mg, Dietary Fiber: 2.5 g, Fat: 10 g, Carbs: 15 g, Protein: 20 g

Pumpkin & Chicken Digestive Delight

A comforting blend of chicken and pumpkin, great for dogs with sensitive stomachs and digestive issues.

Yield:	Time to Prepare:	Time to Cook:
6 cups	15 minutes	6 - 8 hours

Ingredients:

- 3 cups (1 ½ pounds) boneless, skinless chicken breasts
- 1 cup pumpkin puree (unsweetened)
- ¾ cup diced carrots
- ¾ cup chopped green beans
- ¾ cup brown rice
- 3 cups low-sodium chicken broth
- 1 ½ tablespoons flaxseed oil
- ½ teaspoon ground ginger
- ½ tablespoon powdered cuttlebone (for calcium)

Instructions:

1) Add chicken, pumpkin, carrots, green beans, and brown rice to the slow cooker.
2) Pour in chicken broth, then add flaxseed oil, ground ginger, and powdered cuttlebone.
3) Stir thoroughly to mix all ingredients.
4) Cover and cook on low for 6 - 8 hours.
5) Shred the chicken and stir well before serving.
6) Allow the food to cool completely before feeding your dog.
7) Store leftovers in an airtight container in the refrigerator for up to 3 days.

Nutritional info per 1 Cup:
Calories: 200, Sodium: 32 mg, Dietary Fiber: 2.5 g, Fat: 7.5 g, Carbs: 15 g, Protein: 18 g

All-In-One Beef & Veggie Feast

A complete and balanced meal featuring lean beef and a colorful array of vegetables, perfect for daily feeding.

Yield:	Time to Prepare:	Time to Cook:
6 cups	**15 minutes**	**6 - 8 hours**

Ingredients:

- 3 cups (1 ½ pounds) ground beef
- ¾ cup diced sweet potatoes
- ¾ cup chopped broccoli
- ¾ cup diced apples (core removed)
- ¾ cup quinoa
- 3 cups low-sodium beef broth
- 1 ½ tablespoons coconut oil
- ½ teaspoon dried basil
- ½ tablespoon ground sesame seeds (for calcium)

Instructions:

1) Place beef, sweet potatoes, broccoli, apples, and quinoa into the slow cooker.
2) Add beef broth, coconut oil, basil, and ground sesame seeds.
3) Stir well to combine all ingredients.
4) Cover and cook on low for 6 - 8 hours.
5) Mix thoroughly and allow it to cool before serving.
6) Store leftovers in the refrigerator for up to 3 days.

Nutritional Info per 1 Cup:
Calories: 225, Sodium: 38 mg, Dietary Fiber: 2.6 g, Fat: 10 g, Carbs: 16 g, Protein: 20 g

Rapid Lamb & Barley Mix

A wholesome lamb and barley dish, great for dogs needing a gentle yet filling meal.

Yield:	Time to Prepare:	Time to Cook:
6 cups	15 minutes	6 - 8 hours

Ingredients:

3 cups (1 ½ pounds) ground lamb

¾ cup pearl barley

¾ cup diced carrots

¾ cup chopped kale

3 cups low-sodium chicken broth

1 ½ tablespoons olive oil

½ teaspoon dried rosemary

½ tablespoon ground crab shell powder (for calcium)

Instructions:

1) Place lamb, barley, carrots, and kale into the slow cooker.
2) Pour in chicken broth, add olive oil, rosemary, and ground crab shell powder.
3) Stir thoroughly to mix all ingredients.
4) Cover and cook on low for 6 - 8 hours.
5) Let the mixture cool before serving.
6) Store leftovers in the refrigerator for up to 3 days.

Nutritional info per 1 Cup:
Calories: 260, Sodium: 45 mg, Dietary Fiber: 2.8 g, Fat: 12 g, Carbs: 18 g, Protein: 20 g

Salmon & Veggie Omega Bowl

A nutrient-packed blend of salmon and mixed vegetables, rich in omega-3s for a shiny coat.

Yield:	Time to Prepare:	Time to Cook:
6 cups	10 minutes	4 - 6 hours

Ingredients:

- 3 cups (1 ½ pounds) boneless, skinless salmon fillets
- ¾ cup chopped spinach
- ¾ cup diced zucchini
- ¾ cup quinoa
- 3 cups water
- 1 ½ tablespoons flaxseed oil
- ½ teaspoon dried dill
- ½ tablespoon powdered cuttlebone (for calcium)

Instructions:

1) Add salmon, spinach, zucchini, and quinoa to the slow cooker.
2) Pour in water, then add flaxseed oil, dill, and powdered cuttlebone.
3) Stir thoroughly to combine all ingredients.
4) Cover and cook on low for 4 - 6 hours.
5) Flake the salmon and mix well before serving.
6) Let it cool before feeding your dog.
7) Store leftovers in the refrigerator for up to 2 days.

Nutritional info per 1 Cup:
Calories: 240, Sodium: 35 mg, Dietary Fiber: 2.1 g, Fat: 10 g, Carbs: 16 g, Protein: 22 g

Turkey & Sweet Potato Sensation

A delicious blend of lean turkey and sweet potatoes, great for dogs who need a boost in fiber.

Yield:	Time to Prepare:	Time to Cook:
6 cups	15 minutes	6 - 8 hours

Ingredients:

3 cups (1 ½ pounds) ground turkey

1 cup diced sweet potatoes

¾ cup diced green beans

¾ cup brown rice

3 cups water

1 ½ tablespoons flaxseed oil

½ teaspoon dried parsley

½ tablespoon ground sunflower seeds (for calcium)

Instructions:

1) Place turkey, sweet potatoes, green beans, and brown rice in the slow cooker.
2) Pour in water, then add flaxseed oil, parsley, and ground sunflower seeds.
3) Stir to combine all ingredients.
4) Cover and cook on low for 6 - 8 hours.
5) Let the mixture cool before serving.
6) Store leftovers in the refrigerator for up to 3 days.

Nutritional info per 1 Cup:
Calories: 215, Sodium: 36 mg, Dietary Fiber: 2 g, Fat: 8 g, Carbs: 15 g, Protein: 19 g

Pork & Pear Hearty Harvest

A delightful blend of lean pork and sweet pears, providing a natural source of vitamins and fiber.

Yield:	Time to Prepare:	Time to Cook:
6 cups	15 minutes	6 - 8 hours

Ingredients:

3 cups (1 ½ pounds) lean ground pork

¾ cup diced pears (core removed)

¾ cup diced sweet potatoes

¾ cup quinoa

3 cups water

1 ½ tablespoons coconut oil

½ teaspoon ground cinnamon

½ tablespoon crushed coral calcium (for calcium)

Instructions:

1) Combine pork, pears, sweet potatoes, and quinoa in the slow cooker.
2) Add water, coconut oil, cinnamon, and crushed coral calcium.
3) Stir thoroughly to mix all ingredients.
4) Cover and cook on low for 6 - 8 hours.
5) Let the mixture cool before serving.
6) Store leftovers in the refrigerator for up to 3 days.

Nutritional info per 1 Cup:
Calories: 220, Sodium: 35 mg, Dietary Fiber: 2.3 g, Fat: 9 g, Carbs: 15 g, Protein: 19 g

Bark & Bite Beefy Lentil Stew

A protein-rich stew with lean beef and lentils, offering a boost in fiber and sustained energy for active dogs.

Yield:	Time to Prepare:	Time to Cook:
6 cups	15 minutes	6 - 8 hours

Ingredients:

- 3 cups (1 ½ pounds) ground beef
- ¾ cup dried green lentils
- ¾ cup diced carrots
- ¾ cup chopped kale
- ¾ cup diced sweet potatoes
- 3 cups low-sodium beef broth
- 1 ½ tablespoons olive oil
- ½ teaspoon dried thyme
- ½ tablespoon ground sardine bones (for calcium)

Instructions:

1) Combine beef, lentils, carrots, kale, and sweet potatoes in the slow cooker.
2) Add beef broth, olive oil, thyme, and ground sardine bones.
3) Stir thoroughly to mix all ingredients.
4) Cover and cook on low for 6 - 8 hours.
5) Stir well before serving and allow it to cool completely.
6) Store leftovers in the refrigerator for up to 4 days.

Nutritional info per 1 Cup:
Calories: 260, Sodium: 42 mg, Dietary Fiber: 2.8 g, Fat: 10 g, Carbs: 18 g, Protein: 21 g

Turkey & Spinach Super Mix

A balanced turkey and spinach recipe designed to support immune health and overall vitality.

Yield:	Time to Prepare:	Time to Cook:
6 cups	10 minutes	6 - 8 hours

Ingredients:

3 cups (1 ½ pounds) ground turkey

¾ cup chopped spinach

¾ cup diced zucchini

¾ cup brown rice

3 cups low-sodium chicken broth

1 ½ tablespoons flaxseed oil

½ teaspoon dried oregano

½ tablespoon ground dried eggshells (for calcium)

Instructions:

1) Place turkey, spinach, zucchini, and brown rice in the slow cooker.
2) Pour in chicken broth, add flaxseed oil, oregano, and ground dried eggshells.
3) Stir well to combine all ingredients.
4) Cover and cook on low for 6 - 8 hours.
5) Mix thoroughly and let the food cool before serving.
6) Store leftovers in an airtight container in the refrigerator for up to 3 days.

Nutritional info per 1 Cup:
Calories: 220, Sodium: 35 mg, Dietary Fiber: 2.2 g, Fat: 9 g, Carbs: 16 g, Protein: 19 g

Salmon & Kale Omega Boost

A tasty, nutrient-dense recipe featuring salmon and kale, rich in omega-3s for skin and coat health.

Yield:	Time to Prepare:	Time to Cook:
6 cups	10 minutes	4 - 6 hours

Ingredients:

3 cups (1 ½ pounds) boneless, skinless salmon fillets

¾ cup chopped kale

¾ cup diced carrots

¾ cup quinoa

3 cups water

1 ½ tablespoons flaxseed oil

½ teaspoon dried dill

½ tablespoon powdered cuttlefish bone (for calcium)

Instructions:

1) Add salmon, kale, carrots, and quinoa to the slow cooker.
2) Pour in water, then add flaxseed oil, dill, and powdered cuttlefish bone.
3) Stir thoroughly to mix.
4) Cover and cook on low for 4 - 6 hours.
5) Flake the salmon and stir well before serving.
6) Allow the food to cool before feeding your dog.
7) Store leftovers in an airtight container for up to 2 days.

Nutritional info per 1 Cup:
Calories: 240, Sodium: 35 mg, Dietary Fiber: 2.1 g, Fat: 10 g, Carbs: 16 g, Protein: 22 g

Chicken & Sweet Pea Supreme

A lean and flavorful dish with chicken and sweet peas, perfect for daily feeding.

Yield:	Time to Prepare:	Time to Cook:
6 cups	15 minutes	6 - 8 hours

Ingredients:

- 3 cups (1 ½ pounds) boneless, skinless chicken thighs
- ¾ cup sweet peas
- ¾ cup diced carrots
- ¾ cup brown rice
- 3 cups low-sodium chicken broth
- 1 ½ tablespoons olive oil
- ½ teaspoon ground turmeric
- ½ tablespoon crushed oyster shells (for calcium

Instructions:

1) Place chicken, sweet peas, carrots, and brown rice in the slow cooker.
2) Pour in chicken broth, then add olive oil, turmeric, and crushed oyster shells.
3) Stir thoroughly and cover to cook on low for 6 - 8 hours.
4) Shred the chicken and mix well before serving.
5) Let the food cool completely before feeding.
6) Store leftovers in the refrigerator for up to 3 days.

Nutritional info per 1 Cup:
Calories: 210, Sodium: 35 mg, Dietary Fiber: 2 g, Fat: 8 g, Carbs: 15 g, Protein: 18 g

Lamb & Lentil Power Bowl

A hearty lamb and lentil dish, offering a great source of protein and fiber for muscle support and digestion.

Yield:	Time to Prepare:	Time to Cook:
6 cups	20 minutes	6 - 8 hours

Ingredients:

- 3 cups (1 ½ pounds) lean ground lamb
- ¾ cup dried lentils
- ¾ cup diced carrots
- ¾ cup chopped spinach
- 3 cups low-sodium chicken broth
- 1 ½ tablespoons coconut oil
- ½ teaspoon dried rosemary
- ½ tablespoon ground eggshell powder (for calcium)

Instructions:

1) Add lamb, lentils, carrots, and spinach to the slow cooker.
2) Pour in chicken broth, then add coconut oil, rosemary, and ground eggshell powder.
3) Stir well to mix all ingredients.
4) Cover and cook on low for 6 - 8 hours.
5) Mix thoroughly and allow it to cool before serving.
6) Store leftovers in the refrigerator for up to 3 days.

Nutritional info per 1 Cup:
Calories: 240, Sodium: 40 mg, Dietary Fiber: 2.5 g, Fat: 10 g, Carbs: 16 g, Protein: 20 g

11

Grain-Free & Gluten-Free Options

Grain-Free Gobbler's Delight

A hearty turkey-based meal, perfect for dogs with grain sensitivities.

Yield:	Time to Prepare:	Time to Cook:
6 cups	15 minutes	6 - 8 hours

Ingredients:

- 3 cups (1 ½ pounds) ground turkey
- ¾ cup diced sweet potatoes
- ¾ cup chopped spinach
- ¾ cup diced carrots
- ¾ cup green beans
- 3 cups low-sodium chicken broth
- 1 ½ tablespoons olive oil
- ½ teaspoon dried rosemary
- ½ crushed eggshell (for calcium)

Instructions:

1) Place ground turkey, sweet potatoes, spinach, carrots, and green beans into the slow cooker.
2) Pour in the chicken broth.
3) Add olive oil, dried rosemary, and crushed eggshell.
4) Stir to combine all ingredients.
5) Cover and cook on low for 6 - 8 hours.
6) Allow the mixture to cool before serving.
7) Store leftovers in the refrigerator for up to 3 days.

Nutritional info per 1 Cup:
Calories: 200, Sodium: 45 mg, Dietary Fiber: 2.5 g, Fat: 8 g, Carbs: 13 g, Protein: 20 g

Sweet Potato Salmon Sensation

Rich in omega-3 fatty acids, this dish promotes a healthy coat and skin.

Yield:	Time to Prepare:	Time to Cook:
6 cups	10 minutes	4 - 6 hours

Ingredients:

- 3 cups (1 ½ pounds) boneless, skinless salmon fillets
- ¾ cup diced sweet potatoes
- ¾ cup chopped broccoli
- ¾ cup diced zucchini
- 3 cups water
- 1 ½ tablespoons flaxseed oil
- ½ teaspoon dried dill
- ½ crushed eggshell (for calcium)

Instructions:

1) Add salmon, sweet potatoes, broccoli, and zucchini to the slow cooker.
2) Pour in water.
3) Add flaxseed oil, dried dill, and crushed eggshell.
4) Stir to combine.
5) Cover and cook on low for 4 - 6 hours.
6) Flake the salmon and mix thoroughly.
7) Let it cool before serving.
8) Store leftovers in the refrigerator for up to 2 days.

Nutritional info per 1 Cup:
Calories: 230, Sodium: 40 mg, Dietary Fiber: 1.8 g, Fat: 10 g, Carbs: 12 g, Protein: 25 g

Pumpkin & Turkey Primal Feast

A grain-free, nutrient-dense meal combining lean turkey and fiber-rich pumpkin.

Yield:	Time to Prepare:	Time to Cook:
6 cups	15 minutes	6 - 8 hours

Ingredients:

- 3 cups (1 ½ pounds) ground turkey
- ¾ cup pumpkin puree (unsweetened)
- ¾ cup diced carrots
- ¾ cup chopped kale
- ¾ cup green peas
- 3 cups low-sodium chicken broth
- 1 ½ tablespoons coconut oil
- ½ teaspoon ground turmeric
- ½ crushed eggshell (for calcium)

Instructions:

1) Place ground turkey, pumpkin puree, carrots, kale, and green peas into the slow cooker.
2) Pour in the chicken broth.
3) Add coconut oil, ground turmeric, and crushed eggshell.
4) Stir to combine all ingredients.
5) Cover and cook on low for 6 - 8 hours.
6) Allow the mixture to cool before serving.
7) Store leftovers in the refrigerator for up to 3 days.

Nutritional info per 1 Cup:
Calories: 220, Sodium: 40 mg, Dietary Fiber: 2.5 g, Fat: 9 g, Carbs: 12 g, Protein: 22 g

Pawsome Paleo Pork & Apple Stew

A delightful blend of pork and apples, offering a grain-free, paleo-friendly option.

Yield:	Time to Prepare:	Time to Cook:
6 cups	20 minutes	6 - 8 hours

Ingredients:

3 cups (1 ½ pounds) lean pork shoulder, cubed

¾ cup diced apples (core removed)

¾ cup diced butternut squash

¾ cup chopped spinach

3 cups low-sodium chicken broth

1 ½ tablespoons olive oil

½ teaspoon dried sage

½ crushed eggshell (for calcium)

Instructions:

1) Add cubed pork, apples, butternut squash, and spinach to the slow cooker.
2) Pour in the chicken broth.
3) Add olive oil, dried sage, and crushed eggshell.
4) Stir to combine all ingredients.
5) Cover and cook on low for 6 - 8 hours.
6) Let it cool before serving.
7) Store leftovers in the refrigerator for up to 3 days.

Nutritional info per 1 Cup:
Calories: 240, Sodium: 40 mg, Dietary Fiber: 1.8 g, Fat: 10 g, Carbs: 13 g, Protein: 22 g

Coconut Chicken Grain-Free Comfort

A creamy, grain-free chicken dish infused with the goodness of coconut.

Yield:	Time to Prepare:	Time to Cook:
6 cups	15 minutes	6 - 8 hours

Ingredients:

- 3 cups (1 ½ pounds) boneless, skinless chicken thighs
- ¾ cup diced sweet potatoes
- ¾ cup chopped green beans
- ¾ cup diced carrots
- ¾ cup coconut milk (unsweetened)
- 2 ½ cups low-sodium chicken broth
- 1 ½ tablespoons coconut oil
- ½ teaspoon ground ginger
- ½ crushed eggshell (for calcium)

Instructions:

1) Place chicken thighs, sweet potatoes, green beans, and carrots into the slow cooker.
2) Pour in coconut milk and chicken broth.
3) Add coconut oil, ground ginger, and crushed eggshell.
4) Stir to combine all ingredients.
5) Cover and cook on low for 6 - 8 hours.
6) Shred the chicken and mix thoroughly.
7) Allow the mixture to cool before serving.
8) Store leftovers in the refrigerator for up to 3 days.

Nutritional info per 1 Cup:
Calories: 225, Sodium: 32 mg, Dietary Fiber: 1.8 g, Fat: 11 g, Carbs: 12 g, Protein: 18 g

Veggie-Loaded Beef Paleo Stew

A hearty, grain-free beef stew packed with nutrient-rich vegetables, perfect for dogs on a paleo-inspired diet.

Yield:	Time to Prepare:	Time to Cook:
6 cups	20 minutes	6 - 8 hours

Ingredients:

- 3 cups (1 ½ pounds) lean beef stew meat, cubed
- ¾ cup diced zucchini
- ¾ cup chopped broccoli
- ¾ cup diced carrots
- ¾ cup diced celery
- 3 cups low-sodium beef broth
- 1 ½ tablespoons coconut oil
- ½ teaspoon dried thyme
- ½ teaspoon ground turmeric
- ½ crushed eggshell (for calcium)

Instructions:

1) Place beef cubes, zucchini, broccoli, carrots, and celery into the slow cooker.
2) Pour in the beef broth, then add coconut oil, thyme, turmeric, and crushed eggshell.
3) Stir thoroughly to mix all ingredients.
4) Cover and cook on low for 6 - 8 hours. Stir occasionally if possible.
5) Check that the beef is tender before serving.
6) Let the stew cool completely before feeding your dog.
7) Store leftovers in an airtight container in the refrigerator for up to 4 days.

Nutritional info per 1 Cup:
Calories: 240, Sodium: 40 mg, Dietary Fiber: 2.2 g, Fat: 11 g, Carbs: 13 g, Protein: 22 g

Quinoa-Free Kale & Cod Casserole

A light and protein-rich meal featuring cod and kale, perfect for grain-sensitive dogs.

Yield:	Time to Prepare:	Time to Cook:
6 cups	15 minutes	4 - 6 hours

Ingredients:

- 3 cups (1 ½ pounds) boneless, skinless cod fillets
- ¾ cup chopped kale
- ¾ cup diced sweet potatoes
- ¾ cup diced carrots
- 3 cups water
- 1 ½ tablespoons olive oil
- ½ teaspoon dried dill
- ½ crushed eggshell (for calcium)

Instructions:

1) Place cod fillets, kale, sweet potatoes, and carrots into the slow cooker.
2) Add water, olive oil, dried dill, and crushed eggshell.
3) Stir thoroughly to mix all ingredients.
4) Cover and cook on low for 4 - 6 hours.
5) Flake the cod and stir well before serving.
6) Let the food cool completely before feeding your dog.
7) Store leftovers in the refrigerator for up to 2 days.

Nutritional info per 1 Cup:
Calories: 200, Sodium: 30 mg, Dietary Fiber: 1.5 g, Fat: 9 g, Carbs: 12 g, Protein: 20 g

Gluten-Free Turkey & Blueberry Boost

A delicious blend of lean turkey and antioxidant-rich blueberries for immune support.

Yield:	Time to Prepare:	Time to Cook:
6 cups	10 minutes	6 - 8 hours

Ingredients:

- 3 cups (1 ½ pounds) ground turkey
- ¾ cup fresh blueberries
- ¾ cup diced zucchini
- ¾ cup chopped spinach
- ¾ cup sweet peas
- 3 cups low-sodium chicken broth
- 1 ½ tablespoons flaxseed oil
- ½ teaspoon dried parsley
- ½ crushed eggshell (for calcium)

Instructions:

1) Add ground turkey, blueberries, zucchini, spinach, and sweet peas to the slow cooker.
2) Pour in chicken broth, then add flaxseed oil, dried parsley, and crushed eggshell.
3) Stir well to combine.
4) Cover and cook on low for 6 - 8 hours.
5) Allow the food to cool before serving.
6) Store leftovers in an airtight container in the refrigerator for up to 3 days.

Nutritional info per 1 Cup:
Calories: 190, Sodium: 28 mg, Dietary Fiber: 1.8 g, Fat: 7 g, Carbs: 11 g, Protein: 18 g

Cranberry Chicken Caveman Chow

A tangy and grain-free dish featuring cranberries and chicken for a flavorful, paleo-inspired meal.

Yield:	Time to Prepare:	Time to Cook:
6 cups	15 minutes	6 - 8 hours

Ingredients:

- 3 cups (1 ½ pounds) boneless, skinless chicken thighs
- ¾ cup fresh cranberries
- ¾ cup diced carrots
- ¾ cup chopped broccoli
- 3 cups low-sodium chicken broth
- 1 ½ tablespoons coconut oil
- ½ teaspoon dried thyme
- ½ crushed eggshell (for calcium)

Instructions:

1) Place chicken thighs, cranberries, carrots, and broccoli in the slow cooker.
2) Add chicken broth, coconut oil, thyme, and crushed eggshell.
3) Stir thoroughly to mix all ingredients.
4) Cover and cook on low for 6 - 8 hours.
5) Shred the chicken and stir well before serving.
6) Let it cool completely before feeding.
7) Store leftovers in the refrigerator for up to 3 days.

Nutritional info per 1 Cup:
Calories: 210, Sodium: 30 mg, Dietary Fiber: 2.2 g, Fat: 9 g, Carbs: 12 g, Protein: 18 g

Pea & Lamb Protein-Packed Bowl

A high-protein, grain-free meal featuring lamb and peas, great for muscle development.

Yield:	Time to Prepare:	Time to Cook:
6 cups	20 minutes	6 - 8 hours

Ingredients:

- 3 cups (1 ½ pounds) ground lamb
- ¾ cup sweet peas
- ¾ cup diced carrots
- ¾ cup chopped spinach
- 3 cups low-sodium chicken broth
- 1 ½ tablespoons olive oil
- ½ teaspoon ground rosemary
- ½ crushed eggshell (for calcium)

Instructions:

1) Add ground lamb, peas, carrots, and spinach to the slow cooker.
2) Pour in chicken broth, then add olive oil, rosemary, and crushed eggshell.
3) Stir well to mix all ingredients.
4) Cover and cook on low for 6 - 8 hours.
5) Mix thoroughly before serving and allow it to cool.
6) Store leftovers in the refrigerator for up to 3 days.

Nutritional info per 1 Cup: Calories: 250, Sodium: 38 mg, Dietary Fiber: 2.5 g, Fat: 10 g, Carbs: 13 g, Protein: 22 g

No-Grain Beef & Spinach Supreme

A rich, grain-free beef recipe with spinach, perfect for dogs on a restricted diet.

Yield:	Time to Prepare:	Time to Cook:
6 cups	15 minutes	6 - 8 hours

Ingredients:

3 cups (1 ½ pounds) ground beef

¾ cup chopped spinach

¾ cup diced carrots

¾ cup green beans

3 cups low-sodium beef broth

1 ½ tablespoons coconut oil

½ teaspoon dried basil

½ crushed eggshell (for calcium)

Instructions:

1) Place ground beef, spinach, carrots, and green beans into the slow cooker.
2) Add beef broth, coconut oil, basil, and crushed eggshell.
3) Stir thoroughly and cover to cook on low for 6 - 8 hours.
4) Let the food cool before serving.
5) Store leftovers in an airtight container for up to 4 days.

Nutritional info per 1 Cup:
Calories: 240, Sodium: 42 mg, Dietary Fiber: 2 g, Fat: 12 g, Carbs: 12 g, Protein: 20 g

Wild Salmon & Butternut Squash Bake

A delicious, omega-rich recipe featuring wild-caught salmon and butternut squash.

Yield:	Time to Prepare:	Time to Cook:
6 cups	10 minutes	4 - 6 hours

Ingredients:

3 cups (1 ½ pounds) boneless, skinless salmon fillets

1 cup diced butternut squash

¾ cup chopped kale

3 cups water

1 ½ tablespoons flaxseed oil

½ teaspoon dried dill

½ crushed eggshell (for calcium)

Instructions:

1) Add salmon, butternut squash, and kale to the slow cooker.
2) Pour in water, then add flaxseed oil, dill, and crushed eggshell.
3) Stir well and cover to cook on low for 4 - 6 hours.
4) Flake the salmon and mix thoroughly.
5) Let the food cool before serving.
6) Store leftovers in the refrigerator for up to 2 days.

Nutritional Info per 1 Cup:
Calories: 230, Sodium: 35 mg, Dietary Fiber: 1.8 g, Fat: 10 g, Carbs: 12 g, Protein: 22 g

Carrot-Coconut Paleo Power Stew

A creamy and grain-free dish infused with coconut and packed with vitamins for a healthy coat.

Yield:	Time to Prepare:	Time to Cook:
6 cups	15 minutes	6 - 8 hours

Ingredients:

- 3 cups (1 ½ pounds) boneless, skinless chicken thighs
- ¾ cup diced carrots
- ¾ cup chopped spinach
- ¾ cup diced zucchini
- ¾ cup unsweetened coconut milk
- 2 ½ cups low-sodium chicken broth
- 1 ½ tablespoons coconut oil
- ½ teaspoon ground turmeric
- ½ crushed eggshell (for calcium)

Instructions:

1) Add chicken thighs, carrots, spinach, and zucchini to the slow cooker.
2) Pour in coconut milk and chicken broth.
3) Add coconut oil, ground turmeric, and crushed eggshell.
4) Stir well to combine all ingredients.
5) Cover and cook on low for 6 - 8 hours.
6) Shred the chicken and mix thoroughly.
7) Let it cool completely before serving.
8) Store leftovers in an airtight container for up to 3 days.

Nutritional info per 1 Cup:
Calories: 210, Sodium: 30 mg, Dietary Fiber: 2 g, Fat: 9 g, Carbs: 11 g, Protein: 19 g

Hunter's Hearty Grain-Free Mix

A savory blend of lean meats and veggies, inspired by a hunter's primal diet.

Yield:	Time to Prepare:	Time to Cook:
6 cups	**20 minutes**	**6 - 8 hours**

Ingredients:

- 1 ½ cups (¾ pound) ground venison
- 1 ½ cups (¾ pound) ground bison
- ¾ cup diced sweet potatoes
- ¾ cup chopped kale
- ¾ cup diced carrots
- 3 cups low-sodium beef broth
- 1 ½ tablespoons olive oil
- ½ teaspoon dried rosemary
- ½ crushed eggshell (for calcium)

Instructions:

1) Add venison, bison, sweet potatoes, kale, and carrots to the slow cooker.
2) Pour in beef broth, then add olive oil, rosemary, and crushed eggshell.
3) Stir well to mix all ingredients.
4) Cover and cook on low for 6 - 8 hours.
5) Mix thoroughly and let the food cool before serving.
6) Store leftovers in the refrigerator for up to 4 days.

Nutritional info per 1 Cup:
Calories: 260, Sodium: 38 mg, Dietary Fiber: 2.5 g, Fat: 12 g, Carbs: 15 g, Protein: 22 g

Sweet Pea & Turkey Caveman Casserole

A simple, grain-free casserole with lean turkey and sweet peas, great for a paleo diet.

Yield:	Time to Prepare:	Time to Cook:
6 cups	15 minutes	6 - 8 hours

Ingredients:

3 cups (1 ½ pounds) ground turkey

¾ cup sweet peas

¾ cup diced carrots

¾ cup diced butternut squash

3 cups low-sodium chicken broth

1 ½ tablespoons coconut oil

½ teaspoon ground sage

½ crushed eggshell (for calcium)

Instructions:

1) Combine ground turkey, sweet peas, carrots, and butternut squash in the slow cooker.
2) Add chicken broth, coconut oil, sage, and crushed eggshell.
3) Stir to mix thoroughly.
4) Cover and cook on low for 6 - 8 hours.
5) Let the casserole cool before serving.
6) Store leftovers in the refrigerator for up to 3 days.

Nutritional info per 1 Cup:
Calories: 230, Sodium: 36 mg, Dietary Fiber: 2 g, Fat: 9 g, Carbs: 13 g, Protein: 21 g

Apple & Pork Paleo Comfort Meal

A tasty and slightly sweet meal combining pork and apples, perfect for a grain-free, paleo-friendly diet.

Yield:	Time to Prepare:	Time to Cook:
6 cups	20 minutes	6 - 8 hours

Ingredients:

3 cups (1 ½ pounds) lean ground pork

¾ cup diced apples (core removed)

¾ cup diced sweet potatoes

¾ cup chopped spinach

3 cups low-sodium chicken broth

1 ½ tablespoons olive oil

½ teaspoon ground cinnamon

½ crushed eggshell (for calcium)

Instructions:

1) Add pork, apples, sweet potatoes, and spinach to the slow cooker.
2) Pour in chicken broth, then add olive oil, cinnamon, and crushed eggshell.
3) Stir well to combine all ingredients.
4) Cover and cook on low for 6 - 8 hours.
5) Let the meal cool before serving.
6) Store leftovers in the refrigerator for up to 3 days.

Nutritional info per 1 Cup:
Calories: 220, Sodium: 35 mg, Dietary Fiber: 2 g, Fat: 10 g, Carbs: 12 g, Protein: 20 g

Wild-Caught Cod & Cauliflower Chowder

A nutrient-packed, grain-free chowder featuring cod and cauliflower for a light, healthy meal.

Yield:	Time to Prepare:	Time to Cook:
6 cups	15 minutes	4 - 6 hours

Ingredients:

- 3 cups (1 ½ pounds) boneless, skinless cod fillets
- ¾ cup chopped cauliflower
- ¾ cup diced zucchini
- ¾ cup diced carrots
- 3 cups water
- 1 ½ tablespoons flaxseed oil
- ½ teaspoon dried dill
- ½ crushed eggshell (for calcium)

Instructions:

1) Add cod, cauliflower, zucchini, and carrots to the slow cooker.
2) Pour in water, then add flaxseed oil, dill, and crushed eggshell.
3) Stir thoroughly to mix.
4) Cover and cook on low for 4 - 6 hours.
5) Flake the cod and stir well before serving.
6) Let the food cool before feeding your dog.
7) Store leftovers in the refrigerator for up to 2 days.

Nutritional info per 1 Cup:
Calories: 200, Sodium: 30 mg, Dietary Fiber: 1.8 g, Fat: 9 g, Carbs: 12 g, Protein: 21 g

Beef & Kale Primal Feast

A protein-packed and grain-free recipe featuring lean beef and kale for a nutrient-dense meal.

Yield:	Time to Prepare:	Time to Cook:
6 cups	20 minutes	6 - 8 hours

Ingredients:

3 cups (1 ½ pounds) ground beef

¾ cup chopped kale

¾ cup diced carrots

¾ cup diced sweet potatoes

3 cups low-sodium beef broth

1 ½ tablespoons coconut oil

½ teaspoon ground thyme

½ crushed eggshell (for calcium)

Instructions:

1) Combine beef, kale, carrots, and sweet potatoes in the slow cooker.
2) Add beef broth, coconut oil, thyme, and crushed eggshell.
3) Stir well to combine.
4) Cover and cook on low for 6 - 8 hours.
5) Allow the mixture to cool before serving.
6) Store leftovers in the refrigerator for up to 4 days.

Nutritional info per 1 Cup:
Calories: 230, Sodium: 42 mg, Dietary Fiber: 2.3 g, Fat: 11 g, Carbs: 12 g, Protein: 20 g

Bone Broth & Pumpkin Paleo Potluck

A comforting, grain-free meal featuring bone broth and pumpkin, perfect for supporting joint health.

Yield:	Time to Prepare:	Time to Cook:
6 cups	15 minutes	6 - 8 hours

Ingredients:

3 cups (1 ½ pounds) boneless, skinless chicken thighs

¾ cup pumpkin puree (unsweetened)

¾ cup diced carrots

¾ cup chopped green beans

2 ½ cups bone broth (low-sodium)

1 ½ tablespoons olive oil

½ teaspoon ground turmeric

½ crushed eggshell (for calcium)

Instructions:

1) Add chicken thighs, pumpkin puree, carrots, and green beans to the slow cooker.
2) Pour in bone broth, then add olive oil, ground turmeric, and crushed eggshell.
3) Stir well to mix all ingredients.
4) Cover and cook on low for 6 - 8 hours.
5) Shred the chicken and mix thoroughly before serving.
6) Allow it to cool completely before feeding your dog.
7) Store leftovers in the refrigerator for up to 3 days.

Nutritional info per 1 Cup:
Calories: 210, Sodium: 30 mg, Dietary Fiber: 2 g, Fat: 9 g, Carbs: 11 g, Protein: 19 g

Herb-Infused Grain-Free Chicken Dinner

A fragrant and flavorful chicken dinner infused with fresh herbs, ideal for dogs with grain sensitivities.

Yield:	Time to Prepare:	Time to Cook:
6 cups	20 minutes	6 - 8 hours

Ingredients:

3 cups (1 ½ pounds) boneless, skinless chicken breasts

¾ cup chopped spinach

¾ cup diced zucchini

¾ cup diced apples (core removed)

3 cups low-sodium chicken broth

1 ½ tablespoons coconut oil

½ teaspoon dried basil

½ teaspoon dried parsley

½ crushed eggshell (for calcium)

Instructions:

1) Add chicken breasts, spinach, zucchini, and diced apples to the slow cooker.
2) Pour in chicken broth, then add coconut oil, basil, parsley, and crushed eggshell.
3) Stir well to combine all ingredients.
4) Cover and cook on low for 6 - 8 hours.
5) Shred the chicken and mix thoroughly.
6) Allow the dish to cool completely before serving.
7) Store leftovers in the refrigerator for up to 3 days.

Nutritional info per 1 Cup:
Calories: 210, Sodium: 30 mg, Dietary Fiber: 1.8 g, Fat: 8 g, Carbs: 12 g, Protein: 18 g

12

Low-Fat & Low-Calorie Meals

Slim & Trim Turkey & Carrot Medley

A low-fat, high-protein dish featuring lean turkey and crunchy carrots, great for weight management.

Yield:	Time to Prepare:	Time to Cook:
6 cups	10 minutes	6 - 8 hours

Ingredients:

3 cups (1 ½ pounds) ground turkey (93% lean)

¾ cup diced carrots

¾ cup chopped spinach

¾ cup diced zucchini

3 cups low-sodium chicken broth

1 ½ tablespoons olive oil

½ teaspoon dried thyme

½ crushed eggshell (for calcium)

Instructions:

1) Place ground turkey, carrots, spinach, and zucchini in the slow cooker.
2) Pour in chicken broth, then add olive oil, thyme, and crushed eggshell.
3) Stir well to combine all ingredients.
4) Cover and cook on low for 6 - 8 hours.
5) Mix thoroughly and let the food cool before serving.
6) Store leftovers in the refrigerator for up to 3 days.

Nutritional info per 1 Cup:
Calories: 180, Sodium: 30 mg, Dietary Fiber: 1.6 g, Fat: 6 g, Carbs: 12 g, Protein: 16 g

Light & Lean Chicken Veggie Bowl

A light and refreshing meal with lean chicken and mixed veggies, perfect for dogs on a diet.

Yield:	Time to Prepare:	Time to Cook:
6 cups	15 minutes	6 - 8 hours

Ingredients:

3 cups (1 ½ pounds) boneless, skinless chicken breasts

¾ cup diced green beans

¾ cup diced carrots

¾ cup chopped broccoli

3 cups water

1 ½ tablespoons flaxseed oil

½ teaspoon dried parsley

½ crushed eggshell (for calcium)

Instructions:

1) Add chicken breasts, green beans, carrots, and broccoli to the slow cooker.
2) Pour in water, then add flaxseed oil, parsley, and crushed eggshell.
3) Stir thoroughly to mix all ingredients.
4) Cover and cook on low for 6 - 8 hours.
5) Shred the chicken and mix well before serving.
6) Let the food cool completely before feeding.
7) Store leftovers in the refrigerator for up to 3 days.

Nutritional info per 1 Cup:
Calories: 180, Sodium: 25 mg, Dietary Fiber: 2.1 g, Fat: 5.8 g, Carbs: 11 g, Protein: 18 g

Calorie-Conscious Beef & Broccoli Blend

A satisfying low-calorie dish featuring lean beef and fiber-rich broccoli, great for dogs with weight concerns.

Yield:	Time to Prepare:	Time to Cook:
6 cups	20 minutes	6 - 8 hours

Ingredients:

- 3 cups (1 ½ pounds) lean ground beef (90% lean)
- ¾ cup chopped broccoli
- ¾ cup diced carrots
- ¾ cup diced sweet potatoes
- 3 cups low-sodium beef broth
- 1 ½ tablespoons olive oil
- ½ teaspoon dried oregano
- ½ crushed eggshell (for calcium)

Instructions:

1) Place ground beef, broccoli, carrots, and sweet potatoes in the slow cooker.
2) Pour in beef broth, add olive oil, oregano, and crushed eggshell.
3) Stir well to mix all ingredients.
4) Cover and cook on low for 6 - 8 hours.
5) Let the food cool before serving.
6) Store leftovers in the refrigerator for up to 4 days.

Nutritional info per 1 Cup:
Calories: 200, Sodium: 40 mg, Dietary Fiber: 2 g, Fat: 9 g, Carbs: 13 g, Protein: 18 g

Skinny Salmon & Spinach Delight

A low-fat, high-omega meal featuring salmon and spinach, supporting healthy weight and a shiny coat.

Yield:	Time to Prepare:	Time to Cook:
6 cups	10 minutes	4 - 6 hours

Ingredients:

- 3 cups (1 ½ pounds) boneless, skinless salmon fillets
- ¾ cup chopped spinach
- ¾ cup diced zucchini
- ¾ cup diced apples (core removed)
- 3 cups water
- 1 ½ tablespoons flaxseed oil
- ½ teaspoon dried dill
- ½ crushed eggshell (for calcium)

Instructions:

1) Add salmon, spinach, zucchini, and apples to the slow cooker.
2) Pour in water, then add flaxseed oil, dill, and crushed eggshell.
3) Stir thoroughly to combine all ingredients.
4) Cover and cook on low for 4 - 6 hours.
5) Flake the salmon and stir well before serving.
6) Allow the food to cool completely before feeding.
7) Store leftovers in the refrigerator for up to 2 days.

Nutritional info per 1 Cup:
Calories: 190, Sodium: 30 mg, Dietary Fiber: 1.8 g, Fat: 7 g, Carbs: 12 g, Protein: 20 g

Lightened-Up Lamb & Lentil Stew

A low-fat, high-protein stew with lean lamb and fiber-rich lentils, great for maintaining a healthy weight.

Yield:	Time to Prepare:	Time to Cook:
6 cups	20 minutes	6 - 8 hours

Ingredients:

3 cups (1 ½ pounds) lean ground lamb

¾ cup dried lentils

¾ cup diced carrots

¾ cup diced sweet potatoes

3 cups low-sodium chicken broth

1 ½ tablespoons coconut oil

½ teaspoon dried rosemary

½ crushed eggshell (for calcium)

Instructions:

1) Combine ground lamb, lentils, carrots, and sweet potatoes in the slow cooker.
2) Add chicken broth, then add coconut oil, rosemary, and crushed eggshell.
3) Stir well to mix all ingredients.
4) Cover and cook on low for 6 - 8 hours.
5) Stir thoroughly before serving and let it cool completely.
6) Store leftovers in the refrigerator for up to 3 days.

Nutritional info per 1 Cup:
Calories: 200, Sodium: 35 mg, Dietary Fiber: 2.8 g, Fat: 8 g, Carbs: 14 g, Protein: 18 g

Guilt-Free Sweet Potato & Apple Treat

A delicious and low-calorie option combining sweet potatoes and apples, great for dogs needing a lighter meal.

Yield:	Time to Prepare:	Time to Cook:
6 cups	15 minutes	6 - 8 hours

Ingredients:

3 cups (1 ½ pounds) boneless, skinless chicken breasts

¾ cup diced sweet potatoes

¾ cup diced apples (core removed)

¾ cup chopped kale

3 cups water

1 ½ tablespoons olive oil

½ teaspoon ground cinnamon

½ crushed eggshell (for calcium)

Instructions:

1) Add chicken breasts, sweet potatoes, apples, and kale to the slow cooker.
2) Pour in water, then add olive oil, cinnamon, and crushed eggshell.
3) Stir well to combine all ingredients.
4) Cover and cook on low for 6 - 8 hours.
5) Shred the chicken and mix thoroughly before serving.
6) Let the food cool completely before feeding.
7) Store leftovers in the refrigerator for up to 3 days.

Nutritional info per 1 Cup:
Calories: 180, Sodium: 30 mg, Dietary Fiber: 2 g, Fat: 7 g, Carbs: 13 g, Protein: 17 g

Skinny Chicken & Zucchini Hash

A low-fat, veggie-packed meal with chicken and zucchini, perfect for dogs on a weight-loss plan.

Yield:	Time to Prepare:	Time to Cook:
6 cups	10 minutes	6 - 8 hours

Ingredients:

- 3 cups (1 ½ pounds) ground chicken (lean)
- ¾ cup diced zucchini
- ¾ cup diced carrots
- ¾ cup chopped spinach
- 3 cups low-sodium chicken broth
- 1 ½ tablespoons flaxseed oil
- ½ teaspoon dried oregano
- ½ crushed eggshell (for calcium)

Instructions:

1) Add ground chicken, zucchini, carrots, and spinach to the slow cooker.
2) Pour in chicken broth, then add flaxseed oil, oregano, and crushed eggshell.
3) Stir thoroughly to mix all ingredients.
4) Cover and cook on low for 6 - 8 hours.
5) Mix well and allow it to cool before serving.
6) Store leftovers in the refrigerator for up to 3 days.

Nutritional info per 1 Cup:
Calories: 180, Sodium: 25 mg, Dietary Fiber: 1.8 g, Fat: 6 g, Carbs: 11 g, Protein: 18 g

Lean Green Bean & Turkey Supreme

A low-calorie, high-fiber turkey dish with green beans, supporting healthy digestion and weight control.

Yield:	Time to Prepare:	Time to Cook:
6 cups	15 minutes	6 - 8 hours

Ingredients:

3 cups (1 ½ pounds) ground turkey (93% lean)

¾ cup chopped green beans

¾ cup diced carrots

¾ cup diced sweet potatoes

3 cups water

1 ½ tablespoons olive oil

½ teaspoon dried basil

½ crushed eggshell (for calcium)

Instructions:

1) Add ground turkey, green beans, carrots, and sweet potatoes to the slow cooker.
2) Pour in water, then add olive oil, basil, and crushed eggshell.
3) Stir well to combine all ingredients.
4) Cover and cook on low for 6 - 8 hours.
5) Mix thoroughly and let it cool before serving.
6) Store leftovers in the refrigerator for up to 4 days.

Nutritional info per 1 Cup:
Calories: 190, Sodium: 30 mg, Dietary Fiber: 2.3 g, Fat: 7 g, Carbs: 13 g, Protein: 17 g

Low-Calorie Cod & Kale Mash-Up

A light and nutrient-dense recipe with cod and kale, providing essential vitamins without extra calories.

Yield:	Time to Prepare:	Time to Cook:
6 cups	15 minutes	4 - 6 hours

Ingredients:

3 cups (1 ½ pounds) boneless, skinless cod fillets

¾ cup chopped kale

¾ cup diced carrots

¾ cup diced zucchini

3 cups water

1 ½ tablespoons flaxseed oil

½ teaspoon dried dill

½ crushed eggshell (for calcium)

Instructions:

1) Add cod fillets, kale, carrots, and zucchini to the slow cooker.
2) Pour in water, then add flaxseed oil, dill, and crushed eggshell.
3) Stir well to combine all ingredients.
4) Cover and cook on low for 4 - 6 hours.
5) Flake the cod and stir thoroughly before serving.
6) Let it cool before feeding your dog.
7) Store leftovers in the refrigerator for up to 2 days.

Nutritional info per 1 Cup:
Calories: 180, Sodium: 28 mg, Dietary Fiber: 1.5 g, Fat: 7 g, Carbs: 11 g, Protein: 19 g

Svelte Sweet Potato & Pork Mash

A light and filling dish featuring lean pork and fiber-rich sweet potatoes, perfect for dogs needing a lighter meal.

Yield:	Time to Prepare:	Time to Cook:
6 cups	20 minutes	6 - 8 hours

Ingredients:

3 cups (1 ½ pounds) lean ground pork

1 cup diced sweet potatoes

¾ cup diced apples (core removed)

¾ cup chopped spinach

3 cups low-sodium chicken broth

1 ½ tablespoons coconut oil

½ teaspoon ground cinnamon

½ crushed eggshell (for calcium)

Instructions:

1) Combine ground pork, sweet potatoes, apples, and spinach in the slow cooker.
2) Pour in chicken broth, then add coconut oil, cinnamon, and crushed eggshell.
3) Stir well to mix all ingredients.
4) Cover and cook on low for 6 - 8 hours.
5) Mix thoroughly and allow it to cool before serving.
6) Store leftovers in the refrigerator for up to 3 days.

Nutritional info per 1 Cup:
Calories: 190, Sodium: 30 mg, Dietary Fiber: 2 g, Fat: 8 g, Carbs: 13 g, Protein: 18 g

Lite Bite Beef & Pumpkin Platter

A wholesome, low-fat dish combining lean beef and pumpkin, supporting healthy digestion.

Yield:	Time to Prepare:	Time to Cook:
6 cups	15 minutes	6 - 8 hours

Ingredients:

- 3 cups (1 ½ pounds) lean ground beef (90% lean)
- ¾ cup pumpkin puree (unsweetened)
- ¾ cup diced carrots
- ¾ cup chopped green beans
- 3 cups low-sodium beef broth
- 1 ½ tablespoons flaxseed oil
- ½ teaspoon dried rosemary
- ½ crushed eggshell (for calcium)

Instructions:

1) Place ground beef, pumpkin puree, carrots, and green beans in the slow cooker.
2) Pour in beef broth, then add flaxseed oil, rosemary, and crushed eggshell.
3) Stir well to combine all ingredients.
4) Cover and cook on low for 6 - 8 hours.
5) Mix thoroughly and let the food cool before serving.
6) Store leftovers in the refrigerator for up to 4 days.

Nutritional Info per 1 Cup:
Calories: 180, Sodium: 30 mg, Dietary Fiber: 2 g, Fat: 7 g, Carbs: 11 g, Protein: 17 g

Skinny Veggie & Turkey Fit Feast

A light yet satisfying turkey and veggie dish, perfect for weight-conscious dogs.

Yield:	Time to Prepare:	Time to Cook:
6 cups	10 minutes	6 - 8 hours

Ingredients:

- 3 cups (1 ½ pounds) ground turkey (93% lean)
- ¾ cup chopped spinach
- ¾ cup diced zucchini
- ¾ cup diced sweet potatoes
- 3 cups water
- 1 ½ tablespoons coconut oil
- ½ teaspoon dried basil
- ½ crushed eggshell (for calcium)

Instructions:

1) Add ground turkey, spinach, zucchini, and sweet potatoes to the slow cooker.
2) Pour in water, then add coconut oil, basil, and crushed eggshell.
3) Stir well to mix all ingredients.
4) Cover and cook on low for 6 - 8 hours.
5) Mix thoroughly before serving and let it cool completely.
6) Store leftovers in the refrigerator for up to 3 days.

Nutritional info per 1 Cup:
Calories: 170, Sodium: 25 mg, Dietary Fiber: 2 g, Fat: 6 g, Carbs: 12 g, Protein: 15 g

Calorie Cutter Chicken & Apple Mix

A light and flavorful meal featuring lean chicken and apples, providing a low-calorie option with a touch of sweetness.

Yield:	Time to Prepare:	Time to Cook:
6 cups	**15 minutes**	**6 - 8 hours**

Ingredients:

- 3 cups (1 ½ pounds) boneless, skinless chicken breasts
- ¾ cup diced apples (core removed)
- ¾ cup diced carrots
- ¾ cup chopped kale
- 3 cups low-sodium chicken broth
- 1 tablespoon olive oil
- ½ teaspoon ground cinnamon
- ½ crushed eggshell (for calcium)

Instructions:

1) Place chicken, apples, carrots, and kale in the slow cooker.
2) Pour in chicken broth, then add olive oil, cinnamon, and crushed eggshell.
3) Stir well to combine all ingredients.
4) Cover and cook on low for 6 - 8 hours.
5) Shred the chicken and mix thoroughly before serving.
6) Let it cool before feeding.
7) Store leftovers in the refrigerator for up to 3 days.

Nutritional info per 1 Cup:
Calories: 160, Sodium: 20 mg, Dietary Fiber: 1.8 g, Fat: 5 g, Carbs: 10 g, Protein: 14 g

Low-Fat Lamb & Carrot Surprise

A lean lamb and carrot dish designed to provide flavor without the extra calories.

Yield:	Time to Prepare:	Time to Cook:
6 cups	20 minutes	6 - 8 hours

Ingredients:

- 3 cups (1 ½ pounds) ground lamb (lean)
- ¾ cup diced carrots
- ¾ cup diced sweet potatoes
- ¾ cup chopped green beans
- 3 cups water
- 1 ½ tablespoons olive oil
- ½ teaspoon dried thyme
- ½ crushed eggshell (for calcium)

Instructions:

1) Add ground lamb, carrots, sweet potatoes, and green beans to the slow cooker.
2) Pour in water, then add olive oil, thyme, and crushed eggshell.
3) Stir thoroughly to mix all ingredients.
4) Cover and cook on low for 6 - 8 hours.
5) Mix well before serving and let it cool completely.
6) Store leftovers in the refrigerator for up to 3 days.

Nutritional info per 1 Cup:
Calories: 190, Sodium: 30 mg, Dietary Fiber: 2 g, Fat: 8 g, Carbs: 12 g, Protein: 16 g

Wholesome Waistline Chicken Chowder

A low-fat, nutrient-rich chicken chowder that helps support a healthy weight.

Yield:	Time to Prepare:	Time to Cook:
6 cups	15 minutes	6 - 8 hours

Ingredients:

- 3 cups (1 ½ pounds) boneless, skinless chicken thighs
- ¾ cup diced sweet potatoes
- ¾ cup diced celery
- ¾ cup chopped spinach
- 3 cups low-sodium chicken broth
- 1 ½ tablespoons flaxseed oil
- ½ teaspoon dried oregano
- ½ crushed eggshell (for calcium)

Instructions:

1) Place chicken thighs, sweet potatoes, celery, and spinach in the slow cooker.
2) Pour in chicken broth, then add flaxseed oil, oregano, and crushed eggshell.
3) Stir well to combine all ingredients.
4) Cover and cook on low for 6 - 8 hours.
5) Shred the chicken and mix thoroughly before serving.
6) Allow it to cool completely before feeding.
7) Store leftovers in the refrigerator for up to 3 days.

Nutritional info per 1 Cup:
Calories: 170, Sodium: 25 mg, Dietary Fiber: 1.5 g, Fat: 6 g, Carbs: 10 g, Protein: 15 g

Lean Green Turkey & Pea Stew

A quick and light turkey stew featuring green peas, providing a great low-calorie option.

Yield:	Time to Prepare:	Time to Cook:
6 cups	10 minutes	6 - 8 hours

Ingredients:

3 cups (1 ½ pounds) ground turkey (93% lean)

¾ cup sweet peas

¾ cup diced carrots

¾ cup chopped spinach

3 cups low-sodium chicken broth

1 ½ tablespoons coconut oil

½ teaspoon dried basil

1 tablespoon ground sesame seeds (for calcium)

Instructions:

1) Add ground turkey, sweet peas, carrots, and spinach to the slow cooker.
2) Pour in chicken broth, then add coconut oil, basil, and ground sesame seeds.
3) Stir well to combine all ingredients.
4) Cover and cook on low for 6 - 8 hours.
5) Stir thoroughly before serving and let it cool.
6) Store leftovers in an airtight container in the refrigerator for up to 3 days.

Nutritional info per 1 Cup:
Calories: 180, Sodium: 25 mg, Dietary Fiber: 1.8 g, Fat: 7 g, Carbs: 10 g, Protein: 16 g

Trimmed-Down Beef & Spinach Bowl

A flavorful beef and spinach recipe with a shorter cooking time, ideal for a quick, low-fat meal.

Yield:	Time to Prepare:	Time to Cook:
6 cups	**15 minutes**	**6 - 8 hours**

Ingredients:

- 3 cups (1 ½ pounds) lean ground beef (90% lean)
- ¾ cup chopped spinach
- ¾ cup diced zucchini
- ¾ cup diced apples (core removed)
- 3 cups low-sodium beef broth
- 1 tablespoon olive oil
- ½ teaspoon dried thyme
- 1 tablespoon bone meal powder (for calcium)

Instructions:

1) Place ground beef, spinach, zucchini, and diced apples in the slow cooker.
2) Pour in beef broth, then add olive oil, thyme, and bone meal powder.
3) Stir thoroughly to mix all ingredients.
4) Cover and cook on low for 6 - 8 hours.
5) Allow the food to cool completely before serving.
6) Store leftovers in the refrigerator for up to 3 days.

Nutritional info per 1 Cup:
Calories: 190, Sodium: 30 mg, Dietary Fiber: 2 g, Fat: 7 g, Carbs: 11 g, Protein: 17 g

Slim Salmon & Blueberry Mix

A quick, omega-rich dish combining salmon and antioxidant-packed blueberries, ready in under 3 hours.

Yield:	Time to Prepare:	Time to Cook:
6 cups	10 minutes	4 - 6 hours

Ingredients:

- 3 cups (1 ½ pounds) boneless, skinless salmon fillets
- ¾ cup fresh blueberries
- ¾ cup diced carrots
- ¾ cup chopped kale
- 3 cups water
- 1 tablespoon flaxseed oil
- ½ teaspoon dried dill
- ½ tablespoon crushed oyster shell powder (for calcium)

Instructions:

1) Add salmon fillets, blueberries, carrots, and kale to the slow cooker.
2) Pour in water, then add flaxseed oil, dill, and oyster shell powder.
3) Stir well to combine all ingredients.
4) Cover and cook on low for 4 - 6 hours.
5) Flake the salmon and mix thoroughly before serving.
6) Let the food cool completely before feeding your dog.
7) Store leftovers in the refrigerator for up to 2 days.

Nutritional info per 1 Cup:
Calories: 200, Sodium: 25 mg, Dietary Fiber: 1.6 g, Fat: 8 g, Carbs: 9 g, Protein: 18 g

Low-Cal Lamb & Lentil Love

A fast-cooking lamb and lentil dish, offering high protein and fiber with a shorter cooking time.

Yield:	Time to Prepare:	Time to Cook:
6 cups	15 minutes	6 - 8 hours

Ingredients:

- 3 cups (1 ½ pounds) lean ground lamb
- ¾ cup dried lentils (rinsed)
- ¾ cup diced sweet potatoes
- ¾ cup diced celery
- 3 cups low-sodium chicken broth
- 1 tablespoon coconut oil
- ½ teaspoon dried rosemary
- ½ tablespoon chia seeds (for calcium)

Instructions:

1) Combine ground lamb, lentils, sweet potatoes, and celery in the slow cooker.
2) Pour in chicken broth, then add coconut oil, rosemary, and chia seeds.
3) Stir well to mix all ingredients.
4) Cover and cook on low for 6 - 9 hours.
5) Mix thoroughly and allow it to cool before serving.
6) Store leftovers in the refrigerator for up to 3 days.

Nutritional info per 1 Cup:
Calories: 220, Sodium: 35 mg, Dietary Fiber: 2.5 g, Fat: 9 g, Carbs: 13 g, Protein: 18 g

Lite Liver & Veggie Dinner

A low-fat liver recipe packed with vitamins, offering a nutritious, lighter meal option.

Yield:	Time to Prepare:	Time to Cook:
6 cups	10 minutes	6 - 8 hours

Ingredients:

3 cups (1 ½ pounds) chicken liver (trimmed)

¾ cup diced carrots

¾ cup diced green beans

¾ cup chopped spinach

3 cups low-sodium chicken broth

1 tablespoon olive oil

½ teaspoon dried basil

½ tablespoon ground sesame seeds (for calcium)

Instructions:

1) Add chicken liver, carrots, green beans, and spinach to the slow cooker.
2) Pour in chicken broth, then add olive oil, basil, and ground sesame seeds.
3) Stir thoroughly to mix all ingredients.
4) Cover and cook on low for 6 - 8 hours.
5) Stir well before serving and let the food cool completely.
6) Store leftovers in the refrigerator for up to 3 days.

Nutritional info per 1 Cup:
Calories: 170, Sodium: 30 mg, Dietary Fiber: 1.6 g, Fat: 6 g, Carbs: 10 g, Protein: 15 g

13

Special Health Needs

Sensitive Stomach Sweet Potato & Cod Stew

A gentle and easily digestible recipe, great for dogs with sensitive tummies.

Yield:	Time to Prepare:	Time to Cook:
6 cups	10 minutes	4 - 6 hours

Ingredients:

3 cups (1 ½ pounds) boneless, skinless cod fillets

¾ cup diced sweet potatoes

¾ cup diced fennel

¾ cup chopped spinach

3 cups water

1 tablespoon olive oil

½ teaspoon grated ginger

½ tablespoon crushed eggshell powder (for calcium)

Instructions:

1) Add cod, sweet potatoes, fennel, and spinach to the slow cooker.
2) Pour in water, then add olive oil, grated ginger, and eggshell powder.
3) Stir well to combine.
4) Cover and cook on low for 4 - 6 hours.
5) Flake the cod and mix thoroughly before serving.
6) Let the food cool before feeding your dog.
7) Store leftovers in the refrigerator for up to 2 days.

Nutritional info per 1 Cup:
Calories: 180, Sodium: 28 mg, Dietary Fiber: 1.8 g, Fat: 6 g, Carbs: 12 g, Protein: 20 g

Joint Support Chicken & Pumpkin Blend

A joint-supporting meal rich in collagen from chicken and anti-inflammatory pumpkin.

Yield:	Time to Prepare:	Time to Cook:
6 cups	15 minutes	6 - 8 hours

Ingredients:

- 3 cups (1 ½ pounds) chicken thighs (bone-in, skin removed)
- ¾ cup pumpkin puree (unsweetened)
- ¾ cup diced celery
- ¾ cup diced carrots
- 3 cups low-sodium chicken broth
- 1 tablespoon coconut oil
- ½ teaspoon turmeric
- ½ tablespoon ground flaxseed (for calcium)

Instructions:

1) Place chicken thighs, pumpkin, celery, and carrots in the slow cooker.
2) Pour in chicken broth, then add coconut oil, turmeric, and ground flaxseed.
3) Stir thoroughly to combine all ingredients.
4) Cover and cook on low for 6 - 8 hours.
5) Remove the bones, shred the chicken, and mix well before serving.
6) Let the food cool completely before feeding.
7) Store leftovers in the refrigerator for up to 3 days.

Nutritional info per 1 Cup:
Calories: 200, Sodium: 32 mg, Dietary Fiber: 2 g, Fat: 8 g, Carbs: 10 g, Protein: 18 g

Heart-Healthy Turkey & Beet Bowl

A nutrient-dense meal featuring beets, which support cardiovascular health.

Yield:	Time to Prepare:	Time to Cook:
6 cups	15 minutes	6 - 8 hours

Ingredients:

- 3 cups (1 ½ pounds) ground turkey
- ¾ cup diced beets
- ¾ cup chopped kale
- ¾ cup diced apples (core removed)
- 3 cups water
- 1 ½ tablespoons olive oil
- ½ teaspoon dried oregano
- ½ tablespoon bone meal powder (for calcium)

Instructions:

1) Add ground turkey, beets, kale, and diced apples to the slow cooker.
2) Pour in water, then add olive oil, oregano, and bone meal powder.
3) Stir thoroughly to mix all ingredients.
4) Cover and cook on low for 6 - 8 hours.
5) Mix well before serving and allow it to cool.
6) Store leftovers in an airtight container in the refrigerator for up to 3 days.

Nutritional info per 1 Cup:
Calories: 180, Sodium: 25 mg, Dietary Fiber: 2 g, Fat: 7 g, Carbs: 11 g, Protein: 17 g

Anti-Inflammatory Beef & Turmeric Mash

A soothing recipe for dogs with inflammation, featuring anti-inflammatory turmeric and lean beef.

Yield:	Time to Prepare:	Time to Cook:
6 cups	15 minutes	6 - 8 hours

Ingredients:

- 3 cups (1 ½ pounds) lean ground beef (90% lean)
- ¾ cup diced sweet potatoes
- ¾ cup diced zucchini
- ¾ cup chopped parsley
- 3 cups low-sodium beef broth
- 1 tablespoon coconut oil
- ½ teaspoon turmeric
- ½ tablespoon chia seeds (for calcium)

Instructions:

1) Combine ground beef, sweet potatoes, zucchini, and parsley in the slow cooker.
2) Pour in beef broth, then add coconut oil, turmeric, and chia seeds.
3) Stir well to combine all ingredients.
4) Cover and cook on low for 6 - 8 hours.
5) Mix thoroughly before serving and let the food cool completely.
6) Store leftovers in the refrigerator for up to 3 days.

Nutritional info per 1 Cup:
Calories: 190, Sodium: 30 mg, Dietary Fiber: 2 g, Fat: 8 g, Carbs: 13 g, Protein: 18 g

Skin & Coat Salmon & Flaxseed Feast

An omega-rich recipe featuring salmon and flaxseed, supporting healthy skin and a glossy coat.

Yield:	Time to Prepare:	Time to Cook:
6 cups	10 minutes	4 - 6 hours

Ingredients:

- 3 cups (1 ½ pounds) boneless, skinless salmon fillets
- ¾ cup chopped spinach
- ¾ cup diced carrots
- ¾ cup diced pears (core removed)
- 3 cups water
- 1 tablespoon flaxseed oil
- ½ teaspoon dried dill
- ½ tablespoon sesame seeds (for calcium)

Instructions:

1) Add salmon fillets, spinach, carrots, and pears to the slow cooker.
2) Pour in water, then add flaxseed oil, dill, and sesame seeds.
3) Stir well to mix thoroughly.
4) Cover and cook on low for 4 - 6 hours.
5) Flake the salmon and stir well before serving.
6) Let the food cool completely before feeding.
7) Store leftovers in the refrigerator for up to 2 days.

Nutritional info per 1 Cup:
Calories: 200, Sodium: 25 mg, Dietary Fiber: 1.5 g, Fat: 9 g, Carbs: 10 g, Protein: 18 g

Digestive Boost Pumpkin & Pork Stew

A fiber-rich recipe with pumpkin and lean pork, designed to support digestive health.

Yield:	Time to Prepare:	Time to Cook:
6 cups	15 minutes	6 - 8 hours

Ingredients:

- 3 cups (1 ½ pounds) lean ground pork
- ¾ cup pumpkin puree (unsweetened)
- ¾ cup diced celery
- ¾ cup diced green beans
- 3 cups water
- 1 ½ tablespoons olive oil
- ½ teaspoon grated ginger
- ½ tablespoon ground sunflower seeds (for calcium)

Instructions:

1) Place ground pork, pumpkin puree, celery, and green beans into the slow cooker.
2) Pour in water, then add olive oil, grated ginger, and ground sunflower seeds.
3) Stir well to mix all ingredients.
4) Cover and cook on low for 6 - 8 hours.
5) Mix thoroughly before serving and allow it to cool.
6) Store leftovers in the refrigerator for up to 3 days.

Nutritional info per 1 Cup:
Calories: 190, Sodium: 28 mg, Dietary Fiber: 2.2 g, Fat: 7 g, Carbs: 11 g, Protein: 17 g

Kidney-Friendly Lamb & Quinoa Mix

A low-phosphorus recipe with lamb and quinoa, tailored for dogs with kidney concerns.

Yield:	Time to Prepare:	Time to Cook:
6 cups	**20 minutes**	**6 - 8 hours**

Ingredients:

3 cups (1 ½ pounds) lean ground lamb

¾ cup cooked quinoa

¾ cup diced cauliflower

¾ cup chopped spinach

3 cups low-sodium chicken broth

1 tablespoon coconut oil

½ teaspoon dried oregano

½ tablespoon ground eggshell powder (for calcium)

Instructions:

1) Add ground lamb, cooked quinoa, cauliflower, and spinach to the slow cooker.
2) Pour in chicken broth, then add coconut oil, oregano, and eggshell powder.
3) Stir well to mix thoroughly.
4) Cover and cook on low for 6 - 8 hours.
5) Stir well before serving and allow the food to cool.
6) Store leftovers in the refrigerator for up to 3 days.

Nutritional info per 1 Cup:
Calories: 210, Sodium: 25 mg, Dietary Fiber: 1.8 g, Fat: 9 g, Carbs: 10 g, Protein: 18 g

Low-Allergen Turkey & Green Bean Bowl

A hypoallergenic recipe using turkey and green beans, great for dogs with food sensitivities.

Yield:	Time to Prepare:	Time to Cook:
6 cups	10 minutes	6 - 8 hours

Ingredients:

- 3 cups (1 ½ pounds) ground turkey
- ¾ cup chopped green beans
- ¾ cup diced zucchini
- ¾ cup diced apples (core removed)
- 3 cups water
- 1 tablespoon flaxseed oil
- ½ teaspoon dried thyme
- ½ tablespoon ground chia seeds (for calcium)

Instructions:

1) Add ground turkey, green beans, zucchini, and diced apples to the slow cooker.
2) Pour in water, then add flaxseed oil, thyme, and ground chia seeds.
3) Stir thoroughly to combine all ingredients.
4) Cover and cook on low for 6 - 8 hours.
5) Mix well before serving and let it cool completely.
6) Store leftovers in the refrigerator for up to 3 days.

Nutritional info per 1 Cup:
Calories: 180, Sodium: 22 mg, Dietary Fiber: 1.8 g, Fat: 6 g, Carbs: 9 g, Protein: 15 g

Immune Support Chicken & Kale Blend

A nutrient-packed recipe featuring chicken and kale, providing a boost to the immune system.

Yield:	Time to Prepare:	Time to Cook:
6 cups	15 minutes	6 -8 hours

Ingredients:

- 3 cups (1 ½ pounds) boneless, skinless chicken thighs
- ¾ cup chopped kale
- ¾ cup diced carrots
- ¾ cup diced blueberries
- 3 cups low-sodium chicken broth
- 1 ½ tablespoons olive oil
- ½ teaspoon ground turmeric
- ½ tablespoon crushed oyster shell powder (for calcium)

Instructions:

1) Add chicken thighs, kale, carrots, and blueberries to the slow cooker.
2) Pour in chicken broth, then add olive oil, turmeric, and oyster shell powder.
3) Stir thoroughly to combine all ingredients.
4) Cover and cook on low for 6 - 8 hours.
5) Shred the chicken and mix well before serving.
6) Let it cool completely before feeding your dog.
7) Store leftovers in the refrigerator for up to 3 days.

Nutritional info per 1 Cup:
Calories: 200, Sodium: 22 mg, Dietary Fiber: 2.2 g, Fat: 8 g, Carbs: 10 g. Protein: 18 g

Diabetic-Friendly Beef & Lentil Medley

A high-fiber, low-sugar recipe designed for dogs with diabetes, using lean beef and lentils.

Yield:	Time to Prepare:	Time to Cook:
6 cups	20 minutes	6 - 8 hours

Ingredients:

- 3 cups (1 ½ pounds) lean ground beef
- ¾ cup dried green lentils
- ¾ cup diced butternut squash
- ¾ cup chopped kale
- 3 cups low-sodium beef broth
- 1 tablespoon coconut oil
- ½ teaspoon ground cinnamon
- ½ tablespoon bone meal powder (for calcium)

Instructions:

1) Combine ground beef, lentils, butternut squash, and kale in the slow cooker.
2) Pour in beef broth, then add coconut oil, cinnamon, and bone meal powder.
3) Stir well to mix all ingredients thoroughly.
4) Cover and cook on low for 6 - 8 hours.
5) Stir well before serving and let it cool completely.
6) Store leftovers in the refrigerator for up to 4 days.

Nutritional info per 1 Cup:
Calories: 210, Sodium: 28 mg, Dietary Fiber: 3.5 g, Fat: 8 g, Carbs: 12 g, Protein: 19 g

Liver Care Lamb & Sweet Potato Stew

A liver-friendly recipe featuring lamb and sweet potatoes, tailored for dogs needing liver support.

Yield:	Time to Prepare:	Time to Cook:
5 cups	15 minutes	6 - 8 hours

Ingredients:

- 2 pounds lean ground lamb
- 1 cup diced sweet potatoes
- 1 cup diced beets
- 1 cup chopped spinach
- 3 cups low-sodium chicken broth
- 1 tablespoon olive oil
- 1 teaspoon dried parsley
- 1 tablespoon ground flaxseed (for calcium)

Instructions:

1) Add ground lamb, sweet potatoes, beets, and spinach to the slow cooker.
2) Pour in chicken broth, then add olive oil, parsley, and ground flaxseed.
3) Stir thoroughly to mix all ingredients.
4) Cover and cook on low for 6 - 8 hours.
5) Stir well before serving and allow it to cool completely.
6) Store leftovers in the refrigerator for up to 3 days.

Nutritional info per 1 Cup:
Calories: 190, Sodium: 25 mg, Dietary Fiber: 2.4 g, Fat: 8.5 g, Carbs: 12 g, Protein: 17 g

Omega-Boost Salmon & Chia Supper

A high-omega recipe with salmon and chia seeds, perfect for promoting a shiny coat and healthy skin.

Yield:	Time to Prepare:	Time to Cook:
6 cups	10 minutes	4 - 6 hours

Ingredients:

- 2 pounds boneless, skinless salmon fillets
- 1 cup diced zucchini
- 1 cup chopped kale
- 1 cup diced carrots
- 3 cups water
- 1 tablespoon flaxseed oil
- 1 teaspoon dried dill
- 1 tablespoon chia seeds (for calcium)

Instructions:

1) Add salmon, zucchini, kale, and carrots to the slow cooker.
2) Pour in water, then add flaxseed oil, dill, and chia seeds.
3) Stir well to combine all ingredients.
4) Cover and cook on low for 4 - 6 hours.
5) Flake the salmon and mix thoroughly before serving.
6) Let the food cool completely before feeding your dog.
7) Store leftovers in the refrigerator for up to 2 days.

Nutritional info per 1 Cup:
Calories: 210, Sodium: 20 mg, Dietary Fiber: 1.8 g, Fat: 10 g, Carbs: 10 g, Protein: 20 g

High-Fiber Chicken & Carrot Digestive Delight

A fiber-rich recipe with chicken and carrots, great for promoting healthy digestion.

Yield:	Time to Prepare:	Time to Cook:
6 cups	15 minutes	6 - 8 hours

Ingredients:

2 pounds boneless, skinless chicken breasts

1/2 cup diced carrots

1/2 cup diced celery

1/2 cup diced apples (core removed)

2 cups low-sodium chicken broth

1 tablespoon olive oil

1 teaspoon dried thyme

1 tablespoon crushed oyster shell powder (for calcium)

Instructions:

1) Add chicken, carrots, celery, and apples to the slow cooker.
2) Pour in chicken broth, then add olive oil, thyme, and oyster shell powder.
3) Stir well to mix thoroughly.
4) Cover and cook on low for 6 - 8 hours.
5) Shred the chicken and mix well before serving. Let it cool completely.
6) Store leftovers in the refrigerator for up to 3 days.

Nutritional info per 1 Cup:
Calories: 180, Sodium: 20 mg, Dietary Fiber: 2.2 g, Fat: 6.5 g, Carbs: 9 g, Protein: 18 g

Senior Dog Beef & Pumpkin Comfort Mix

A soft and easily digestible beef and pumpkin mix, perfect for senior dogs with sensitive teeth.

Yield:	Time to Prepare:	Time to Cook:
5 cups	15 minutes	6 - 8 hours

Ingredients:

- 2 pounds lean ground beef
- 1/2 cup pumpkin puree (unsweetened)
- 1/2 cup diced sweet potatoes
- 1/2 cup chopped green beans
- 2 cups low-sodium beef broth
- 1 tablespoon coconut oil
- 1 teaspoon dried rosemary
- 1 tablespoon bone meal powder (for calcium)

Instructions:

1) Add beef, pumpkin puree, sweet potatoes, and green beans to the slow cooker.
2) Pour in beef broth, then add coconut oil, rosemary, and bone meal powder.
3) Stir well to combine all ingredients.
4) Cover and cook on low for 6 - 8 hours.
5) Mix well and let it cool before feeding.
6) Store leftovers in the refrigerator for up to 4 days.

Nutritional info per 1 Cup:
Calories: 210, Sodium: 18 mg, Dietary Fiber: 2 g, Fat: 9 g, Carbs: 10 g, Protein: 20 g

Urinary Support Turkey & Cranberry Stew

A urinary health-focused meal with lean turkey and cranberries, helping to prevent UTIs.

Yield:	Time to Prepare:	Time to Cook:
5 cups	10 minutes	6 - 8 hours

Ingredients:

- 2 pounds ground turkey
- 1/2 cup fresh cranberries
- 1/2 cup diced zucchini
- 1/2 cup diced celery
- 2 cups water
- 1 tablespoon olive oil
- 1 teaspoon ground cinnamon
- 1 tablespoon ground sesame seeds (for calcium)

Instructions:

1) Combine turkey, cranberries, zucchini, and celery in the slow cooker.
2) Pour in water, then add olive oil, cinnamon, and sesame seeds.
3) Stir thoroughly to mix all ingredients.
4) Cover and cook on low for 6 - 8 hours.
5) Stir well before serving and let it cool completely.
6) Store leftovers in the refrigerator for up to 3 days.

Nutritional info per 1 Cup:
Calories: 190, Sodium: 15 mg, Dietary Fiber: 1.9 g, Fat: 8 g, Carbs: 7 g, Protein: 19 g

Allergy Relief Duck-Free Delight

A hypoallergenic, duck-free recipe for dogs with common poultry allergies, featuring lean pork and vegetables.

Yield: 6 cups	Time to Prepare: 10 minutes	Time to Cook: 6 - 8 hours

Ingredients:

- 2 pounds lean ground pork
- 1/2 cup diced butternut squash
- 1/2 cup chopped broccoli
- 1/2 cup diced pears (core removed)
- 2 cups water
- 1 tablespoon coconut oil
- 1 teaspoon dried basil
- 1 tablespoon ground flaxseed (for calcium)

Instructions:

1) Add pork, butternut squash, broccoli, and pears to the slow cooker.
2) Pour in water, then add coconut oil, basil, and flaxseed.
3) Stir thoroughly to combine all ingredients.
4) Cover and cook on low for 6 - 8 hours.
5) Mix well and let the food cool completely before serving.
6) Store leftovers in the refrigerator for up to 3 days.

Nutritional info per 1 Cup:
Calories: 220, Sodium: 25 mg, Dietary Fiber: 2.5 g, Fat: 8.5 g, Carbs: 11 g, Protein: 20 g

Weight Management Pork & Spinach Blend

A low-calorie recipe with lean pork and spinach, perfect for dogs needing to maintain a healthy weight.

Yield:	Time to Prepare:	Time to Cook:
6 cups	10 minutes	6 - 8 hours

Ingredients:

- 2 pounds lean ground pork
- 1/2 cup chopped spinach
- 1/2 cup diced apples (core removed)
- 1/2 cup diced celery
- 2 cups low-sodium chicken broth
- 1 tablespoon olive oil
- 1 teaspoon dried thyme
- 1 tablespoon crushed eggshell powder (for calcium)

Instructions:

1) Add pork, spinach, apples, and celery to the slow cooker.
2) Pour in chicken broth, then add olive oil, thyme, and eggshell powder.
3) Stir well to mix all ingredients.
4) Cover and cook on low for 6 - 8 hours.
5) Stir thoroughly and let the food cool before serving.
6) Store leftovers in the refrigerator for up to 3 days.

Nutritional info per 1 Cup:
Calories: 210, Sodium: 30 mg, Dietary Fiber: 2.2 g, Fat: 9 g, Carbs: 10 g, Protein: 21 g

Bone Health Turkey & Sardine Casserole

A calcium-rich recipe featuring turkey and sardines, supporting strong bones and teeth.

Yield:	Time to Prepare:	Time to Cook:
5 cups	10 minutes	6 - 8 hours

Ingredients:

2 pounds ground turkey

1/2 can sardines in water (drained)

1/2 cup diced zucchini

1/2 cup diced sweet potatoes

2 cups low-sodium chicken broth

1 tablespoon flaxseed oil

1 teaspoon dried rosemary

1 tablespoon bone meal powder (for calcium)

Instructions:

1) Add turkey, sardines, zucchini, and sweet potatoes to the slow cooker.
2) Pour in chicken broth, then add flaxseed oil, rosemary, and bone meal powder.
3) Stir thoroughly to combine all ingredients.
4) Cover and cook on low for 6 - 8 hours.
5) Mix well and let it cool completely before serving.
6) Store leftovers in the refrigerator for up to 3 days.

Nutritional info per 1 Cup:
Calories: 230, Sodium: 28 mg, Dietary Fiber: 1.8 g, Fat: 10 g, Carbs: 9 g, Protein: 23 g

Low-Sodium Chicken & Rice Recovery Meal

A gentle, low-sodium recipe with chicken and rice, perfect for dogs recovering from illness.

Yield:	Time to Prepare:	Time to Cook:
5 cups	10 minutes	6 - 8 hours

Ingredients:

- 2 pounds boneless, skinless chicken breasts
- 1/2 cup cooked white rice
- 1/2 cup diced carrots
- 1/2 cup chopped green beans
- 2 cups water
- 1 tablespoon olive oil
- 1 teaspoon grated ginger
- 1 tablespoon ground sesame seeds (for calcium)

Instructions:

1) Add chicken, cooked rice, carrots, and green beans to the slow cooker.
2) Pour in water, then add olive oil, ginger, and sesame seeds.
3) Stir thoroughly to mix all ingredients.
4) Cover and cook on low for 6 - 8 hours.
5) Shred the chicken and mix well before serving. Let it cool completely.
6) Store leftovers in the refrigerator for up to 3 days.

Nutritional info per 1 Cup:
Calories: 180, Sodium: 18 mg, Dietary Fiber: 1.5 g, Fat: 7 g, Carbs: 10 g, Protein: 20 g

Inflammation Fighter Beef & Blueberry Bowl

A powerful anti-inflammatory recipe combining lean beef and antioxidant-rich blueberries.

Yield:	Time to Prepare:	Time to Cook:
6 cups	**10 minutes**	**6 - 8 hours**

Ingredients:

2 pounds lean ground beef

1/2 cup fresh blueberries

1/2 cup diced sweet potatoes

1/2 cup chopped spinach

2 cups low-sodium beef broth

1 tablespoon coconut oil

1 teaspoon ground turmeric

1 tablespoon chia seeds (for calcium)

Instructions:

1) Add beef, blueberries, sweet potatoes, and spinach to the slow cooker.
2) Pour in beef broth, then add coconut oil, turmeric, and chia seeds.
3) Stir well to mix all ingredients.
4) Cover and cook on low for 6 - 8 hours.
5) Mix thoroughly and let it cool before serving.
6) Store leftovers in the refrigerator for up to 3 days.

Nutritional info per 1 Cup:
Calories: 200, Sodium: 25 mg, Dietary Fiber: 2.5 g, Fat: 9 g, Carbs: 11 g, Protein: 21 g

14

Homemade Biscuits and Chews

Crunchy Carrot & Apple Biscuits

A tasty and crunchy treat with carrots and apples, great for dental health and satisfying snack time.

Yield:	Time to Prepare:	Time to Cook:
20 biscuits	10 minutes	1 hour

Ingredients:

- 1 cup grated carrots
- 1 cup grated apple (core removed)
- 1 ½ cups oat flour
- 1 egg
- 2 tablespoons coconut oil
- 1 teaspoon ground flaxseed (for omega-3s)
- 1 tablespoon powdered eggshell (for calcium)

Instructions:

1) Mix grated carrots, grated apple, oat flour, egg, and coconut oil in a bowl.
1) Add flaxseed and powdered eggshell; stir until dough forms.
2) Shape into small biscuits and place on a baking sheet in the slow cooker.
3) Cover and cook on high for 1 hour or until firm and slightly browned.
4) Cool completely before serving.
5) Store in an airtight container for up to 1 week.

Nutritional info per Biscuit:
Calories: 50, Sodium: 5 mg, Dietary Fiber: 1.2 g, Fat: 2 g, Carbs: 8 g, Protein: 1.5 g

Peanut Butter Banana Bites

A chewy and flavorful treat packed with peanut butter and banana, perfect for training rewards.

Yield:	Time to Prepare:	Time to Cook:
24 bites	10 minutes	1.5 hours

Ingredients:

- 1 ripe banana, mashed
- 1 cup peanut butter (unsweetened, xylitol-free)
- 1 cup rolled oats
- 1 tablespoon chia seeds (for fiber and calcium)
- 1 teaspoon honey (optional)

Instructions:

1) Mix banana, peanut butter, oats, chia seeds, and honey in a bowl.
2) Form into small bite-sized balls and place on a parchment-lined baking sheet in the slow cooker.
3) Cook on high for 1.5 hours until firm.
4) Cool completely before serving.
5) Store in an airtight container for up to 1 week.

Nutritional info per Bite:
Calories: 60, Sodium: 10 mg, Dietary Fiber: 1.5 g, Fat: 3 g, Carbs: 7 g, Protein: 2 g

Sweet Potato Chewies

A simple, natural chew treat made from sweet potatoes, perfect for dogs that need a satisfying chew.

Yield:	Time to Prepare:	Time to Cook:
12 chews	5 minutes	1.5 hours

Ingredients:

2 large sweet potatoes, sliced into thin rounds

1 tablespoon olive oil

1 teaspoon ground turmeric

Instructions:

1) Toss sweet potato slices in olive oil and sprinkle with turmeric.
2) Arrange slices on a baking sheet in the slow cooker.
3) Cook on high for 1.5 hours, flipping halfway, until chewy and slightly crisp.
4) Cool completely before serving.
5) Store in an airtight container for up to 5 days.

Nutritional info per Chew:
Calories: 40, Sodium: 5 mg, Dietary Fiber: 1 g, Fat: 1.5 g, Carbs: 7 g, Protein: 0.5 g

Cheesy Chicken Bites

These savory treats combine chicken and cheese, making them irresistible and protein-packed.

Yield:	Time to Prepare:	Time to Cook:
20 bites	10 minutes	1 hour

Ingredients:

1 cup shredded chicken (cooked)

½ cup shredded cheddar cheese

1 egg

1 cup oat flour

1 tablespoon ground flaxseed (for omega-3s)

Instructions:

1) Combine chicken, cheese, egg, oat flour, and flaxseed in a bowl.
2) Form into small bite-sized balls.
3) Place bites on a baking sheet in the slow cooker.
4) Cook on high for 1 hour until firm.
5) Cool completely before serving.
6) Store in the refrigerator for up to 1 week.

Nutritional info per Bite:
Calories: 70, Sodium: 20 mg, Dietary Fiber: 1 g, Fat: 3 g, Carbs: 5 g, Protein: 4 g

Pumpkin & Parsley Breath Fresheners

A crunchy treat with pumpkin and parsley to help freshen your dog's breath naturally.

Yield:	Time to Prepare:	Time to Cook:
30 treats	10 minutes	1 hour

Ingredients:

1 cup pumpkin puree (unsweetened)

½ cup chopped fresh parsley

1 egg

1 ½ cups oat flour

1 tablespoon powdered kelp (for iodine and calcium)

Instructions:

1) Mix pumpkin, parsley, egg, and oat flour in a bowl.
2) Add powdered kelp and stir until dough forms.
3) Roll into small balls and flatten slightly.
4) Arrange treats on a baking sheet in the slow cooker.
5) Cook on high for 1 hour until firm.
6) Cool completely before serving.
7) Store in an airtight container for up to 1 week.

Nutritional info per Treat:
Calories: 30, Sodium: 8 mg, Dietary Fiber: 1 g, Fat: 1 g, Carbs: 4 g, Protein: 1 g

Apple Cinnamon Crunchies

A delightful crunchy treat combining apple and cinnamon, great for digestion and a sweet, healthy snack.

Yield:	Time to Prepare:	Time to Cook:
24 treats	10 minutes	1 hour

Ingredients:

1 cup grated apple (core removed)

1 cup oat flour

1 egg

1 tablespoon ground flaxseed (for fiber)

1 teaspoon ground cinnamon

1 tablespoon powdered eggshell (for calcium)

Instructions:

1) Mix apple, oat flour, egg, flaxseed, and cinnamon in a bowl.
2) Add powdered eggshell and stir until a dough forms.
3) Shape into small flat treats and place on a parchment-lined baking sheet in the slow cooker.
4) Cook on high for 1 hour until firm and golden brown.
5) Let the treats cool completely before serving.
6) Store in an airtight container for up to 1 week.

Nutritional info per Treat:
Calories: 35, Sodium: 5 mg, Dietary Fiber: 1 g, Fat: 1 g, Carbs: 6 g, Protein: 1.2 g

Blueberry Bliss Bites

Packed with antioxidant-rich blueberries, these chewy treats are great for boosting your dog's immune system.

Yield:	Time to Prepare:	Time to Cook:
20 bites	10 minutes	1 hour

Ingredients:

1 cup fresh blueberries

1 cup rolled oats

½ cup peanut butter (unsweetened, xylitol-free)

1 egg

1 tablespoon chia seeds (for calcium and fiber)

Instructions:

1) Mix blueberries, oats, peanut butter, egg, and chia seeds in a bowl.
2) Form into small bite-sized balls.
3) Place on a baking sheet in the slow cooker.
4) Cook on high for 1 hour until firm.
5) Cool completely before serving.
6) Store in an airtight container for up to 1 week.

Nutritional info per Bite:
Calories: 45, Sodium: 10 mg, Dietary Fiber: 1.2 g, Fat: 2 g, Carbs: 7 g, Protein: 1.5 g

Sweet Potato & Salmon Chews

A savory and satisfying chew treat with sweet potato and salmon, perfect for healthy skin and coat.

Yield:	Time to Prepare:	Time to Cook:
15 chews	10 minutes	1.5 hours

Ingredients:

1 large sweet potato, sliced thinly

½ cup canned salmon (boneless, skinless)

1 tablespoon olive oil

1 teaspoon ground kelp (for calcium and iodine)

Instructions:

1) Mix salmon and olive oil in a bowl.
2) Coat sweet potato slices with the salmon mixture and sprinkle with ground kelp.
3) Arrange slices on a baking sheet in the slow cooker.
4) Cook on high for 1.5 hours until chewy but not hard.
5) Let cool completely before serving.
6) Store leftovers in the refrigerator for up to 5 days.

Nutritional info per Chew:
Calories: 50, Sodium: 15 mg, Dietary Fiber: 1 g, Fat: 2.5 g, Carbs: 6 g, Protein: 2 g

Cheddar & Parsley Breath Biscuits

A savory treat made with cheddar and parsley to help freshen your dog's breath naturally.

Yield:	Time to Prepare:	Time to Cook:
30 biscuits	10 minutes	1 hour

Ingredients:

1 cup shredded cheddar cheese

½ cup chopped fresh parsley

1 cup whole wheat flour

1 egg

1 tablespoon ground flaxseed (for omega-3s)

1 tablespoon ground dried shrimp shells (for calcium)

Instructions:

1) Combine cheese, parsley, flour, egg, flaxseed, and shrimp shells in a bowl.
2) Mix well until a dough forms and shape into small biscuits.
3) Arrange biscuits on a baking sheet in the slow cooker.
4) Cook on high for 1 hour until firm.
5) Cool completely before serving.
6) Store in an airtight container for up to 1 week.

Nutritional info per Biscuit:
Calories: 40, Sodium: 25 mg, Dietary Fiber: 0.8 g, Fat: 2 g, Carbs: 5 g, Protein: 2 g

Pumpkin & Oat Crunchies

These crunchy treats are made with pumpkin and oats, perfect for digestion and a healthy snack.

Yield:	Time to Prepare:	Time to Cook:
24 treats	10 minutes	1 hour

Ingredients:

1 cup pumpkin puree (unsweetened)

1 cup rolled oats

1 egg

1 tablespoon ground chia seeds (for calcium and fiber)

1 teaspoon ground cinnamon

Instructions:

1) Mix pumpkin puree, oats, egg, chia seeds, and cinnamon in a bowl until well combined.
2) Form small balls and flatten slightly.
3) Arrange treats on a baking sheet in the slow cooker.
4) Cook on high for 1 hour until firm and slightly crisp.
5) Cool completely before serving.
6) Store in an airtight container for up to 1 week.

Nutritional info per Treat:
Calories: 35, Sodium: 8 mg, Dietary Fiber: 1.2 g, Fat: 1 g, Carbs: 6 g, Protein: 1 g

15

Special Occasion Treats

Birthday Pupcake Delight

A festive, dog-friendly cupcake perfect for celebrating your furry friend's special day.

Yield:	Time to Prepare:	Time to Cook:
12 pupcakes	15 minutes	1 hour

Ingredients:

- 1 cup whole wheat flour
- 1 cup grated carrots
- 1 mashed banana
- ½ cup unsweetened applesauce
- 1 egg
- 2 tablespoons coconut oil
- 1 teaspoon baking powder
- 1 tablespoon ground eggshell (for calcium)

Instructions:

1) Mix all ingredients in a bowl until well combined.
2) Pour the batter into silicone muffin cups.
3) Place the cups in the slow cooker and cook on high for 1 hour.
4) Let the pupcakes cool completely before serving.
5) Store leftovers in the refrigerator for up to 5 days.

Nutritional info per Pupcake:
Calories: 80, Sodium: 15 mg, Dietary Fiber: 2 g, Fat: 3 g, Carbs: 12 g, Protein: 2 g

Peanut Butter & Pumpkin Party Balls

Bite-sized treats combining the delicious flavors of peanut butter and pumpkin.

Yield:	Time to Prepare:	Time to Cook:
20 balls	10 minutes	1 hour

Ingredients:

1 cup pumpkin puree (unsweetened)

½ cup peanut butter (unsweetened, xylitol-free)

1 cup rolled oats

1 egg

1 tablespoon chia seeds (for calcium)

Instructions:

1) Mix all ingredients in a bowl until a dough forms.
2) Shape into small balls and place on a parchment-lined baking sheet in the slow cooker.
3) Cook on high for 1 hour until firm.
4) Let the treats cool completely before serving.
5) Store in an airtight container for up to 1 week.

Nutritional info per Ball:
Calories: 60, Sodium: 10 mg, Dietary Fiber: 1.5 g, Fat: 3 g, Carbs: 7 g, Protein: 2 g

Apple & Bacon Celebration Bites

A savory treat made with crispy bacon and sweet apple, perfect for special occasions.

Yield:	Time to Prepare:	Time to Cook:
20 bites	10 minutes	1.5 hours

Ingredients:

1 cup diced apple (core removed)

½ cup crumbled cooked bacon (unsalted)

1 cup oat flour

1 egg

1 tablespoon ground flaxseed (for omega-3s)

1 teaspoon ground cinnamon

Instructions:

1) Mix all ingredients in a bowl until combined.
2) Form small bite-sized balls and place them on a baking sheet in the slow cooker.
3) Cook on high for 1.5 hours until firm.
4) Let the bites cool completely before serving.
5) Store in an airtight container for up to 1 week.

Nutritional info per Bite:
Calories: 70, Sodium: 20 mg, Dietary Fiber: 1 g, Fat: 4 g, Carbs: 6 g, Protein: 2 g

Carob & Banana Party Cookies

Cookies with carob, a safe chocolate alternative, and sweet banana for a delicious treat.

Yield:	Time to Prepare:	Time to Cook:
24 cookies	10 minutes	1 hour

Ingredients:

1 mashed banana

1 cup oat flour

2 tablespoons carob powder

1 egg

1 tablespoon coconut oil

1 teaspoon baking powder

1 tablespoon ground sesame seeds (for calcium)

Instructions:

1) Mix all ingredients in a bowl until a dough forms.
2) Shape the dough into small cookies and place on a baking sheet in the slow cooker.
3) Cook on high for 1 hour until firm.
4) Let the cookies cool before serving.
5) Store in an airtight container for up to 1 week.

Nutritional info per Cookie:
Calories: 45, Sodium: 10 mg, Dietary Fiber: 1 g, Fat: 2 g, Carbs: 7 g, Protein: 1 g

Festive Cranberry & Turkey Treats

A festive treat with lean turkey and tart cranberries, perfect for holiday celebrations.

Yield:	Time to Prepare:	Time to Cook:
20 treats	15 minutes	1 hour

Ingredients:

1 cup cooked, shredded turkey

½ cup chopped dried cranberries (unsweetened)

1 cup whole wheat flour

1 egg

1 tablespoon coconut oil

1 teaspoon ground flaxseed (for fiber and omega-3s)

Instructions:

1) Mix all ingredients in a bowl until well combined.
2) Shape into small treats and place on a parchment-lined baking sheet in the slow cooker.
3) Cook on high for 1 hour until firm.
4) Let the treats cool completely before serving.
5) Store in an airtight container for up to 1 week.

Nutritional info per Treat:
Calories: 50, Sodium: 15 mg, Dietary Fiber: 1 g, Fat: 2 g, Carbs: 6 g, Protein: 3 g

Honey & Oat Celebration Bars

Soft and chewy bars made with honey and oats, perfect for special occasions.

Yield:	Time to Prepare:	Time to Cook:
16 bars	10 minutes	1 hour

Ingredients:

1 cup rolled oats

½ cup honey (raw, unsweetened)

1 mashed banana

1 egg

2 tablespoons coconut oil

1 tablespoon ground chia seeds (for calcium and fiber)

Instructions:

1) Mix all ingredients in a bowl until well combined.
2) Pour the mixture into a parchment-lined slow cooker and spread evenly.
3) Cook on high for 1 hour until firm and golden.
4) Let the bars cool completely before cutting into squares.
5) Store in an airtight container for up to 1 week.

Nutritional info per Bar:
Calories: 70, Sodium: 10 mg, Dietary Fiber: 1.5 g, Fat: 3 g, Carbs: 10 g, Protein: 1.5 g

Savory Cheese & Bacon Bites

Savory treats made with real cheese and bacon, perfect for celebrations.

Yield:	Time to Prepare:	Time to Cook:
20 bites	10 minutes	1 hour

Ingredients:

1 cup shredded cheddar cheese

½ cup cooked, crumbled bacon (unsalted)

1 cup whole wheat flour

1 egg

1 tablespoon ground flaxseed (for omega-3s)

1 tablespoon powdered bone meal (for calcium)

Instructions:

1) Mix all ingredients in a bowl until a dough forms.
2) Form bite-sized balls and place on a parchment-lined baking sheet in the slow cooker.
3) Cook on high for 1 hour until firm.
4) Let the bites cool before serving.
5) Store in an airtight container in the refrigerator for up to 5 days.

Nutritional info per Bite:
Calories: 60, Sodium: 20 mg, Dietary Fiber: 0.8 g, Fat: 4 g, Carbs: 5 g, Protein: 2 g

Sweet Potato & Coconut Festive Chews

Chewy treats with sweet potato and coconut, supporting healthy digestion.

Yield:	Time to Prepare:	Time to Cook:
15 chews	5 minutes	1.5 hours

Ingredients:

2 large sweet potatoes, sliced thinly

2 tablespoons coconut oil

1 tablespoon unsweetened shredded coconut

1 teaspoon ground turmeric

Instructions:

1) Toss sweet potato slices in coconut oil and sprinkle with shredded coconut and turmeric.
2) Place slices on a parchment-lined baking sheet in the slow cooker.
3) Cook on high for 1.5 hours until firm but pliable.
4) Let cool before serving.
5) Store leftovers in the refrigerator for up to 1 week.

Nutritional info per Chew:
Calories: 50, Sodium: 5 mg, Dietary Fiber: 1 g, Fat: 2.5 g, Carbs: 7 g, Protein: 0.5 g

Banana & Yogurt Party Drops

Creamy, frozen drops made with banana and yogurt, perfect for hot days or celebrations.

Yield:	Time to Prepare:	Time to Freeze:
30 drops	10 minutes	1 hour

Ingredients:

1 ripe banana, mashed

1 cup plain Greek yogurt (unsweetened)

1 tablespoon ground flaxseed (for fiber)

1 tablespoon crushed eggshell powder (for calcium)

Instructions:

1) Mix all ingredients in a bowl until smooth.
2) Spoon small dollops onto a parchment-lined tray.
3) Freeze for 1 hour until firm.
4) Serve as a chilled treat and store leftovers in the freezer for up to 1 month.

Nutritional info per Drop:
Calories: 20, Sodium: 8 mg, Dietary Fiber: 0.5 g, Fat: 1 g, Carbs: 3 g, Protein: 1 g

Cranberry & Chicken Celebration Bites

Festive treats combining tart cranberries and lean chicken for holiday celebrations.

Yield:	Time to Prepare:	Time to Cook:
20 bites	15 minutes	1 hour

Ingredients:

1 cup cooked, shredded chicken

½ cup chopped dried cranberries (unsweetened)

1 cup rolled oats

1 egg

2 tablespoons coconut oil

1 tablespoon ground chia seeds (for calcium)

Instructions:

1) Mix all ingredients in a bowl until a dough forms.
2) Shape into small bite-sized balls and place on a baking sheet in the slow cooker.
3) Cook on high for 1 hour until firm.
4) Let the bites cool completely before serving.
5) Store in an airtight container for up to 1 week.

Nutritional info per Bite:
Calories: 55, Sodium: 15 mg, Dietary Fiber: 1 g, Fat: 2 g, Carbs: 6 g, Protein: 3 g

Birthday Pupcake Delight

A festive, dog-friendly cupcake perfect for celebrating your furry friend's special day.

Yield:	Time to Prepare:	Time to Cook:
12 pupcakes	15 minutes	1 hour

Ingredients:

1 cup whole wheat flour

1 cup grated carrots

1 mashed banana

½ cup unsweetened applesauce

1 egg

2 tablespoons coconut oil

1 teaspoon baking powder

1 tablespoon ground eggshell (for calcium)

Instructions:

1) Mix all ingredients in a bowl until well combined.
2) Pour the batter into silicone muffin cups.
3) Place the cups in the slow cooker and cook on high for 1 hour.
4) Let the pupcakes cool completely before serving.
5) Store leftovers in the refrigerator for up to 5 days.

Nutritional info per Pupcake:
Calories: 80, Sodium: 15 mg, Dietary Fiber: 2 g, Fat: 3 g, Carbs: 12 g, Protein: 2 g

Peanut Butter & Pumpkin Party Balls

Bite-sized treats combining the delicious flavors of peanut butter and pumpkin.

Yield:	Time to Prepare:	Time to Cook:
20 balls	10 minutes	1 hour

Ingredients:

1 cup pumpkin puree (unsweetened)

½ cup peanut butter (unsweetened, xylitol-free)

1 cup rolled oats

1 egg

1 tablespoon chia seeds (for calcium)

Instructions:

1) Mix all ingredients in a bowl until a dough forms.
2) Shape into small balls and place on a parchment-lined baking sheet in the slow cooker.
3) Cook on high for 1 hour until firm.
4) Let the treats cool completely before serving.
5) Store in an airtight container for up to 1 week.

Nutritional info per Ball:
Calories: 60, Sodium: 10 mg, Dietary Fiber: 1.5 g, Fat: 3 g, Carbs: 7 g, Protein: 2 g

Apple & Bacon Celebration Bites

A savory treat made with crispy bacon and sweet apple, perfect for special occasions.

Yield:	Time to Prepare:	Time to Cook:
20 bites	10 minutes	1.5 hours

Ingredients:

1 cup diced apple (core removed)

½ cup crumbled cooked bacon (unsalted)

1 cup oat flour

1 egg

1 tablespoon ground flaxseed (for omega-3s)

1 teaspoon ground cinnamon

Instructions:

1) Mix all ingredients in a bowl until combined.
2) Form small bite-sized balls and place them on a baking sheet in the slow cooker.
3) Cook on high for 1.5 hours until firm.
4) Let the bites cool completely before serving.
5) Store in an airtight container for up to 1 week.

Nutritional info per Bite:
Calories: 70, Sodium: 20 mg, Dietary Fiber: 1 g, Fat: 4 g, Carbs: 6 g, Protein: 2 g

Carob & Banana Party Cookies

Cookies with carob, a safe chocolate alternative, and sweet banana for a delicious treat.

Yield:	Time to Prepare:	Time to Cook:
24 cookies	10 minutes	1 hour

Ingredients:

1 mashed banana

1 cup oat flour

2 tablespoons carob powder

1 egg

1 tablespoon coconut oil

1 teaspoon baking powder

1 tablespoon ground sesame seeds (for calcium)

Instructions:

1) Mix all ingredients in a bowl until a dough forms.
2) Shape the dough into small cookies and place on a baking sheet in the slow cooker.
3) Cook on high for 1 hour until firm.
4) Let the cookies cool before serving.
5) Store in an airtight container for up to 1 week.

Nutritional info per Cookie:
Calories: 45, Sodium: 10 mg, Dietary Fiber: 1 g, Fat: 2 g, Carbs: 7 g, Protein: 1 g

Festive Cranberry & Turkey Treats

A festive treat with lean turkey and tart cranberries, perfect for holiday celebrations.

Yield:	Time to Prepare:	Time to Cook:
20 treats	15 minutes	1 hour

Ingredients:

1 cup cooked, shredded turkey

½ cup chopped dried cranberries (unsweetened)

1 cup whole wheat flour

1 egg

1 tablespoon coconut oil

1 teaspoon ground flaxseed (for fiber and omega-3s)

Instructions:

1) Mix all ingredients in a bowl until well combined.
2) Shape into small treats and place on a parchment-lined baking sheet in the slow cooker.
3) Cook on high for 1 hour until firm.
4) Let the treats cool completely before serving.
5) Store in an airtight container for up to 1 week.

Nutritional info per Treat:
Calories: 50, Sodium: 15 mg, Dietary Fiber: 1 g, Fat: 2 g, Carbs: 6 g, Protein: 3 g

Honey & Oat Celebration Bars

Soft and chewy bars made with honey and oats, perfect for special occasions.

Yield:	Time to Prepare:	Time to Cook:
16 bars	**10 minutes**	**1 hour**

Ingredients:

1 cup rolled oats

½ cup honey (raw, unsweetened)

1 mashed banana

1 egg

2 tablespoons coconut oil

1 tablespoon ground chia seeds (for calcium and fiber)

Instructions:

1) Mix all ingredients in a bowl until well combined.
2) Pour the mixture into a parchment-lined slow cooker and spread evenly.
3) Cook on high for 1 hour until firm and golden.
4) Let the bars cool completely before cutting into squares.
5) Store in an airtight container for up to 1 week.

Nutritional info per Bar:
Calories: 70, Sodium: 10 mg, Dietary Fiber: 1.5 g, Fat: 3 g, Carbs: 10 g, Protein: 1.5 g

Savory Cheese & Bacon Bites

Savory treats made with real cheese and bacon, perfect for celebrations.

Yield:	Time to Prepare:	Time to Cook:
20 bites	10 minutes	1 hour

Ingredients:

1 cup shredded cheddar cheese

½ cup cooked, crumbled bacon (unsalted)

1 cup whole wheat flour

1 egg

1 tablespoon ground flaxseed (for omega-3s)

1 tablespoon powdered bone meal (for calcium)

Instructions:

1) Mix all ingredients in a bowl until a dough forms.
2) Form bite-sized balls and place on a parchment-lined baking sheet in the slow cooker.
3) Cook on high for 1 hour until firm.
4) Let the bites cool before serving.
5) Store in an airtight container in the refrigerator for up to 5 days.

Nutritional info per Bite:
Calories: 60, Sodium: 20 mg, Dietary Fiber: 0.8 g, Fat: 4 g, Carbs: 5 g, Protein: 2 g

Sweet Potato & Coconut Festive Chews

Chewy treats with sweet potato and coconut, supporting healthy digestion.

Yield:	Time to Prepare:	Time to Cook:
15 chews	5 minutes	1.5 hours

Ingredients:

2 large sweet potatoes, sliced thinly

2 tablespoons coconut oil

1 tablespoon unsweetened shredded coconut

1 teaspoon ground turmeric

Instructions:

1) Toss sweet potato slices in coconut oil and sprinkle with shredded coconut and turmeric.
2) Place slices on a parchment-lined baking sheet in the slow cooker.
3) Cook on high for 1.5 hours until firm but pliable.
4) Let cool before serving.
5) Store leftovers in the refrigerator for up to 1 week.

Nutritional info per Chew:
Calories: 50, Sodium: 5 mg, Dietary Fiber: 1 g, Fat: 2.5 g, Carbs: 7 g, Protein: 0.5 g

Banana & Yogurt Party Drops

Creamy, frozen drops made with banana and yogurt, perfect for hot days or celebrations.

Yield:	Time to Prepare:	Time to Freeze:
30 drops	10 minutes	1 hour

Ingredients:

1 ripe banana, mashed

1 cup plain Greek yogurt (unsweetened)

1 tablespoon ground flaxseed (for fiber)

1 tablespoon crushed eggshell powder (for calcium)

Instructions:

6) Mix all ingredients in a bowl until smooth.
7) Spoon small dollops onto a parchment-lined tray.
8) Freeze for 1 hour until firm.
9) Serve as a chilled treat and store leftovers in the freezer for up to 1 month.

Nutritional info per Drop:
Calories: 20, Sodium: 8 mg, Dietary Fiber: 0.5 g, Fat: 1 g, Carbs: 3 g, Protein: 1 g

Cranberry & Chicken Celebration Bites

Festive treats combining tart cranberries and lean chicken for holiday celebrations.

Yield:	Time to Prepare:	Time to Cook:
20 bites	15 minutes	1 hour

Ingredients:

1 cup cooked, shredded chicken

½ cup chopped dried cranberries (unsweetened)

1 cup rolled oats

1 egg

2 tablespoons coconut oil

1 tablespoon ground chia seeds (for calcium)

Instructions:

1) Mix all ingredients in a bowl until a dough forms.
2) Shape into small bite-sized balls and place on a baking sheet in the slow cooker.
3) Cook on high for 1 hour until firm.
4) Let the bites cool completely before serving.
5) Store in an airtight container for up to 1 week.

Nutritional info per Bite:
Calories: 55, Sodium: 15 mg, Dietary Fiber: 1 g, Fat: 2 g, Carbs: 6 g, Protein: 3

16

Training Rewards and Snacks

Chicken & Cheese Training Tidbits

Small, protein-packed treats made with chicken and cheese, ideal for training.

Yield:	Prep Time:	Cook Time:
40 tidbits	10 minutes	1 hour

Ingredients:

1 cup shredded cooked chicken

½ cup shredded cheddar cheese

1 egg

1 cup oat flour

1 tablespoon ground chia seeds (for calcium)

Instructions:

1) Combine all ingredients in a bowl and mix well.
2) Form the mixture into small, bite-sized pieces.
3) Place the tidbits on a parchment-lined baking sheet in the slow cooker.
4) Cook on high for 1 hour until firm.
5) Let cool completely before serving as training treats.
6) Store in the refrigerator for up to 1 week.

Nutritional info per Tidbit:
Calories: 15, Sodium: 10 mg, Dietary Fiber: 0.5 g, Fat: 1 g, Carbs: 1 g, Protein: 2 g

Peanut Butter & Carrot Nibbles

Crunchy training snacks with peanut butter and carrot for a healthy reward.

Yield:	Prep Time:	Cook Time:
50 nibbles	10 minutes	1 hour

Ingredients:

1 cup grated carrot

½ cup peanut butter (unsweetened, xylitol-free)

1 egg

1 cup whole wheat flour

1 tablespoon ground flaxseed (for omega-3s)

Instructions:

1) Combine all ingredients in a bowl until a dough forms.
2) Roll the dough into small balls and place on a baking sheet in the slow cooker.
3) Cook on high for 1 hour until firm.
4) Allow the nibbles to cool completely before serving.
5) Store in an airtight container for up to 1 week.

Nutritional info per Nibble:
Calories: 10, Sodium: 5 mg, Dietary Fiber: 0.5 g, Fat: 0.5 g, Carbs: 1 g, Protein: 1 g

Turkey & Blueberry Mini Bites

Antioxidant-rich treats combining turkey and blueberries for nutritious training snacks.

Yield:	Prep Time:	Cook Time:
40 mini bites	10 minutes	1 hour

Ingredients:

1 cup ground turkey (cooked)

½ cup fresh blueberries

1 egg

1 cup rolled oats

1 tablespoon ground eggshell (for calcium)

Instructions:

1) Mix all ingredients in a bowl.
2) Form into small, bite-sized balls and place on a parchment-lined baking sheet in the slow cooker.
3) Cook on high for 1 hour until firm.
4) Let cool before serving.
5) Store in the refrigerator for up to 1 week.

Nutritional info per mini Bite:
Calories: 12, Sodium: 5 mg, Dietary Fiber: 0.5 g, Fat: 0.5 g, Carbs: 1.5 g, Protein: 1.5 g

Salmon & Sweet Potato Training Treats

Packed with omega-3s from salmon and fiber from sweet potatoes for healthy training rewards.

Yield:	Prep Time:	Cook Time:
50 treats	10 minutes	1 hour

Ingredients:

1 cup mashed sweet potato

½ cup canned salmon (boneless, skinless)

1 egg

1 cup oat flour

1 tablespoon ground flaxseed (for omega-3s)

Instructions:

1) Mix all ingredients in a bowl.
2) Form into small, bite-sized pieces and place on a baking sheet in the slow cooker.
3) Cook on high for 1 hour until firm.
4) Allow to cool before serving.
5) Store in an airtight container for up to 1 week.

Nutritional info per Treat:
Calories: 14, Sodium: 8 mg, Dietary Fiber: 0.5 g, Fat: 0.5 g, Carbs: 2 g, Protein: 1 g

Apple & Pumpkin Training Nuggets

Soft and chewy nuggets with apple and pumpkin, ideal for training.

Yield:	Prep Time:	Cook Time:
40 nuggets	10 minutes	1 hour

Ingredients:

1 cup pumpkin puree (unsweetened)

1 grated apple (core removed)

1 egg

1 cup whole wheat flour

1 tablespoon chia seeds (for calcium and fiber)

Instructions:

1) Combine all ingredients in a bowl.
2) Form into small nuggets and place on a baking sheet in the slow cooker.
3) Cook on high for 1 hour until firm.
4) Cool before serving.
5) Store in the refrigerator for up to 1 week.

Nutritional info per Nugget:
Calories: 12, Sodium: 5 mg, Dietary Fiber: 0.5 g, Fat: 0.5 g, Carbs: 2 g, Protein: 1 g

Coconut & Banana Training Bites

A tropical training treat made with coconut and banana, perfect for quick rewards.

Yield:	Prep Time:	Cook Time:
40 bites	10 minutes	1 hour

Ingredients:

1 ripe banana, mashed

1 cup unsweetened shredded coconut

1 egg

1 cup oat flour

1 tablespoon ground chia seeds (for calcium)

Instructions:

1) Combine all ingredients in a bowl and mix thoroughly.
2) Form into small, bite-sized balls and place on a parchment-lined baking sheet in the slow cooker.
3) Cook on high for 1 hour until firm.
4) Cool completely before serving.
5) Store in an airtight container for up to 1 week.

Nutritional info per Bite:
Calories: 15, Sodium: 5 mg, Dietary Fiber: 0.5 g, Fat: 1 g, Carbs: 2 g, Protein: 0.5 g

Beef & Carrot Mini Morsels

Protein-packed treats with beef and carrots for a healthy, savory snack.

Yield:	Prep Time:	Cook Time:
50 morsels	**10 minutes**	**1 hour**

Ingredients:

1 cup lean ground beef (cooked)

1 cup grated carrot

1 egg

1 cup rolled oats

1 tablespoon ground flaxseed (for omega-3s)

Instructions:

1) Mix all ingredients in a bowl.
2) Form into small morsels and place on a baking sheet in the slow cooker.
3) Cook on high for 1 hour until firm.
4) Cool completely before serving.
5) Store in the refrigerator for up to 1 week.

Nutritional info per Morsel:
Calories: 12, Sodium: 8 mg, Dietary Fiber: 0.5 g, Fat: 0.5 g, Carbs: 1.5 g, Protein: 1.5 g

Sweet Potato & Peanut Butter Training Tots

Chewy treats made with sweet potato and peanut butter, great for rewarding good behavior.

Yield:	Prep Time:	Cook Time:
40 tots	10 minutes	1 hour

Ingredients:

1 cup mashed sweet potato

½ cup peanut butter (unsweetened, xylitol-free)

1 egg

1 cup whole wheat flour

1 tablespoon ground sunflower seeds (for calcium)

Instructions:

1) Mix all ingredients in a bowl until combined.
2) Form small tots and place on a baking sheet in the slow cooker.
3) Cook on high for 1 hour until firm.
4) Let cool before serving.
5) Store in an airtight container for up to 1 week.

Nutritional info per Tot:
Calories: 15, Sodium: 10 mg, Dietary Fiber: 0.5 g, Fat: 1 g, Carbs: 2 g, Protein: 1 g

Turkey & Cranberry Nibbles

Festive treats with turkey and cranberries for a delicious training snack.

Yield:	Prep Time:	Cook Time:
50 nibbles	15 minutes	1 hour

Ingredients:

1 cup cooked, shredded turkey

½ cup chopped dried cranberries (unsweetened)

1 egg

1 cup rolled oats

1 tablespoon crushed coral calcium (for calcium)

Instructions:

1) Mix all ingredients in a bowl.
2) Form into small nibbles and place on a parchment-lined baking sheet in the slow cooker.
3) Cook on high for 1 hour until firm.
4) Cool completely before serving.
5) Store in the refrigerator for up to 1 week.

Nutritional info per Nibble:
Calories: 14, Sodium: 7 mg, Dietary Fiber: 0.5 g, Fat: 0.5 g, Carbs: 2 g, Protein: 1.5 g

Pumpkin & Apple Training Bites

Sweet, chewy treats made with pumpkin and apple, perfect for training rewards.

Yield:	Prep Time:	Cook Time:
40 bites	10 minutes	1 hour

Ingredients:

1 cup pumpkin puree (unsweetened)

1 cup grated apple (core removed)

1 egg

1 cup oat flour

1 tablespoon powdered kelp (for calcium and iodine)

Instructions:

1) Mix all ingredients in a bowl until combined.
2) Form into small, bite-sized pieces and place on a baking sheet in the slow cooker.
3) Cook on high for 1 hour until firm.
4) Cool completely before serving.
5) Store in an airtight container for up to 1 week.

Nutritional info per Bite:
Calories: 12, Sodium: 5 mg, Dietary Fiber: 0.5 g, Fat: 0.5 g, Carbs: 2 g, Protein: 1 g

Glossary

Antioxidants: Beneficial compounds that help shield cells from harm.

Balanced diet: A diet that has the right nutrients in the right proportions to support energy, health, biological processes, and growth.

Balanced and complete diet: A term on food labels that indicates it meets AAFCO's minimum nutritional profile.

Carbohydrates: A nutrient that provides energy and aids healthy digestion.

Fats: A nutrient vital for absorbing certain vitamins, providing energy for biological processes, and maintaining skin and coat health.

Fiber: A water-soluble or insoluble carbohydrate needed to maintain the digestive system and regulate the bowels.

Macronutrients: Fats, proteins, and carbohydrates which are needed in large amounts in a dog's diet.

Micronutrients: These nutrients include vitamins and minerals that your dog needs for health but in smaller quantities than macronutrients.

Prebiotics and probiotics: Helpful bacteria that play a role in healthy immunity and digestion.

Protein: A nutrient consisting of various amino acids needed for building, repairing, and maintaining tissues and facilitating a healthy immune system.

References

AAFCO nutrient requirements for dogs. (2021, October 22). *Pet Cubes*. https://www.petcubes.com/blogs/aafco-approved-dog-food/nutrient-requirements

Aaron, M. (2022, September 4). How to make dog food taste better (so picky eaters eat it)? Doggy Saurus. https://doggysaurus.com/how-to-make-dog-food-taste-better/

Bennett, E. (2020, March 31). Our tips for batch cooking and freezing food. Consumer NZ. https://www.consumer.org.nz/articles/batch-cooking-tips-and-getting-the-most-out-of-your-freezer

Calorie ranges for an average healthy adult dog in ideal body condition* Weight (kg) Weight (lb) Kilocalories/day Weight (kg) Weight (lb) Kilocalories/day. (n.d.). WSAVA https://wsava.org/wp-content/uploads/2020/07/Calorie-Needs-for-Healthy-Adult-Dogs-updated-July-2020.pdf

Dumay, M. (2021, April 12). Benefits of slow cookers: 10 reasons to use them. Oven Spot. https://ovenspot.com/benefits-of-slow-cookers/

Eskew, S. (2001, April 17). Fat, protein and carb levels in dog food. Whole Dog Journal. https://www.whole-dog-journal.com/food/fat-protein-and-carb-levels-in-dog-food/

The facts on fiber in dog food. (n.d.). American Kennel Club. https://www.akc.org/expert-advice/nutrition/what-is-fiber-and-why-does-your-dog-need-it-in-their-diet/

Global nutrition guidelines. (n.d.). WSAVA. https://wsava.org/global-guidelines/global-nutrition-guidelines/

Gus. (2016, October 22). 15 slow cooker tips to help you achieve slow cooking perfection. Slow Cooking Perfected. https://slowcookingperfected.com/slow-cooker-tips/

How your dog's nutrition needs change with age. (2018, September 20). www.royalcanin.com.

https://www.royalcanin.com/uk/dogs/health-and-wellbeing/how-your-dogs-nutrition-needs-change-with-age

Hudnell, M. (2021, February 26). Diets for dogs with allergies and sensitivities. Earthborn Holistic Pet Food.

https://www.earthbornholisticpetfood.com/blog/pet-nutrition/diets-for-dogs-with-allergies-and-sensitivities/

The Importance of hydration. (2024). Better Dog. https://wearebetterdog.com/pages/the-imporance-of-hydration

Kevin. (2023, July 23). Enhancing flavors in dog food: A comprehensive guide to safe and Effective Flavor Enhancers - Pet Food Palatant. Pet Food Palatant. https://profypet.com/enhancing-flavors-in-dog-food-a-comprehensive-guide-to-safe-and-effective-flavor-enhancers/

Kim, J. (2024, August 27). Dog nutrition: 6 vet-approved essential nutrients they need. Dogster. https://www.dogster.com/dog-nutrition/dog-nutrients

NRC nutritional requirements for dogs, dog nutrition, raw feeding. (n.d.). Perfectly Rawsome.

https://perfectlyrawsome.com/raw-feeding-knowledgebase/nrc-nutritional-requirements-for-adult-dogs/

Nunez, K. (2023). 7 common mistakes to avoid when using your slow cooker, according to Chefs. Martha Stewart. https://www.marthastewart.com/slow-cooker-mistakes-7968680

Petrenko, I. (2023, October 15). Deliciously allergy-free: Homemade dog food recipes for allergies. Dog Care Journey. https://dogcarejourney.com/dog-food-recipes-for-allergies/

Understanding the unique nutritional needs of different dog breeds. (2023, March 19). Dog Foods Advisor. https://dogfoodsadvisor.com/nutritional-needs-of-different-dog-breeds/

Villasenor, Y. (2017, August 17). The top 7 most common food allergens for dogs. The DogPeople.https://www.rover.com/blog/7-common-food-allergens-dogs/?msockid=172bf6 0e15656a362794e4b514176ba6

Printed in Dunstable, United Kingdom